Delicious and Doable

Desserts

KATIE LEE WILKEN

TEN PEAKS PRESS®
EUGENE, OR

The Scripture quotation is from the American Standard Version of the Bible.

Published in association with Joy Eggerichs Reed of Punchline Agency.

Cover design by Nicole Dougherty
Interior design by Faceout Studio, Paul Nielsen
Food photography by Katie Lee Wilken. Lifestyle photography by Kinsey Whidby.
Graphics © Vodoleyka / Shutterstock

Neither the author nor publisher is responsible for any outcome from use of this cookbook. The recipes are intended for informational purposes and those who have the appropriate culinary skills. USDA guidelines should always be followed in food preparation. The author and publisher make no warranty, express or implied, in any recipe.

TEN PEAKS PRESS is a federally registered trademark of the Hawkins Children's LLC. Harvest House Publishers, Inc., is the exclusive licensee of this trademark.

Delicious and Doable Desserts

Copyright © 2026 by Katie Lee Wilken
Published by Ten Peaks Press, an imprint of Harvest House Publishers
Eugene, Oregon 97408

ISBN 978-0-7369-9113-1 (hardcover)
ISBN 978-0-7369-9114-8 (eBook)

Library of Congress Control Number: 2025939334

No part of this book may be used or reproduced in any manner for the purpose of training artificial intelligence technologies or systems.

All rights reserved. No part of this publication may be reproduced, stored in a retrieval system, or transmitted in any form or by any means—electronic, mechanical, digital, photocopy, recording, or any other—except for brief quotations in printed reviews, without the prior permission of the publisher.

Printed in China

25 26 27 28 29 30 31 32 33 34 / DC / 10 9 8 7 6 5 4 3 2 1

To Grandma Wilken

When I was asked in preschool what I wanted to be when I grew up, I answered, "A grandma." You taught me how to read, introduced me to the joy of baking, and inspired me to become a teacher. You faithfully planted seeds in my life so generously, even though you didn't get to watch them grow for long. God used you in a mighty way in my life. I love you, Grandma.

[CONTENTS]

CHAPTER 1 | Simple Celebrations 7

CHAPTER 2 | Birthdays [FUSS-FREE LAYER CAKES] 29

Write a Meaningful Birthday Card 50

Simple Birthday Decor 52

My Birthday Nonnegotiables 53

CHAPTER 3 | Love [DESSERTS FOR TWO] 55

Simple Ways to Make Your Partner Feel Special 74

CHAPTER 4 | Village People [NOSTALGIC DESSERTS] 77

Throw Together an Easy Montage Video 98

Celebrate the Memory of Someone Special 100

CHAPTER 5 | Major Milestones [SHOWSTOPPING DESSERTS] 103

Host a Honey Roast 124

Create a Surprise Retirement Memory Book 125

CHAPTER 6 | The Little Things [30-MINUTE MASTERPIECES] 127

Establish Your Go-to Dessert 146

Raise a Glass (or a Mug) 147

CHAPTER 7 | Getting Out and Living Life [PORTABLE TREATS] 149

Tips to Package and Transport Desserts 167

CHAPTER 8 | Slow Mornings Together [BREAKFAST SWEETS] 169

"This Is Us" Morning Picture or Video 189

CHAPTER 9 | Building Community [SHARABLE SHEET PAN DESSERTS] 191

The Only Party Game You Will Ever Need! 207

CHAPTER 10 | Not So Basic "Basics" 209

Acknowledgments 221

Index 222

CHAPTER 1

Simple Celebrations

Down six miles of gravel and behind a crowd of pine trees is the ranch I grew up on and where my family still lives. Some might say that I grew up "in the middle of nowhere." The ranch is 30 miles from the nearest "decent-size town" of fewer than 500 people. In fact, where I grew up is the farthest you can get away from a McDonald's in the nation.

When I was five, my mom, dad, sisters Ann and Tricia, and I lived in a simple trailer house. We girls would walk barefoot across the stepping stones leading from our back door over to our grandma and grandad's ranch-style home. Our parents always told us to knock before we wandered into their house, but we would often forget. They welcomed us regardless. This was a simple time, and we didn't go many places besides church and school. My sisters and I spent our time playing house, bathing our cats (poor Jojo), and hanging around our grandparents' house.

Despite our distance from civilization and our uncomplicated life, we were not deprived of celebration. My grandparents led our family in prioritizing celebrating people. These memorable get-togethers would sometimes be just my immediate family, but often would include my aunts, uncles, cousins, and neighbors. Everyone would gather around their dark polished wood table filled with roast beef, potatoes, carrots, salad, and buns. We would all bow our heads and my grandad would pray. He always started his prayer with, "Lord, we thank You for Your many blessings," and during the prayer he would thank God for whomever we were celebrating, whether for a birthday or some other reason.

We would then share a meal and visit. "Visiting" is one of my family's strongest skills. If the Olympics ever add it as an event, the Wilkens will surely get a gold. A good visit usually starts with the weather and works its way from there. After a while my grandma would pull out a dessert—usually her strawberry shortcake—to celebrate the guest of honor. She would light birthday candles and we would all sing. The conversation would quiet as everyone enjoyed the perfect combination of yellow cake, sliced juicy strawberries, and plenty of Cool Whip and ice cream. While these celebrations were nothing over the top, they focused on connection and making the honoree feel loved.

Back to the Beginning

My earliest baking memories were with Grandma Wilken shaping buns in her kitchen, and it only grew from there. I would drag a stack of cookbooks to bed with me and read them cover to cover as I fell asleep. My mom would rarely let me bake, as she had plenty to do raising five girls without cleaning up after a messy baker. So I got most of my baking experience from working alongside my grandma. Slowly, as I got better at cleaning up the kitchen, my mom would give me more opportunities to bake. Nearly every time I got a chance in the kitchen, I tried a new recipe, and it was always a sweet treat. My love of baking and my love of celebrating grew intertwined.

I had caught the bug for celebration, but I wanted it to be impressive and over the top, going against the simple celebrations I grew up on. I have been a party-planning junkie from a young age. I remember searching the Oriental Trading Company catalog for party favors and loving all the little details in picking a party theme. In middle school I fell in love with the look of fondant cakes. I thought they were beautiful and wanted to create one for every family birthday. I don't think anyone in my family actually liked to eat these cakes because of all the fondant—me included! The old saying is true: "We eat with our eyes first." Yet I would add that we also eat with our mouths, so no matter how pretty it looks, it's the taste that is "king."

One evening when I was in high school, I was sitting in the computer lab. (Yes, evening! I went to a boarding school in high school.) Someone told me about a new website I should look at. She instructed me to type the letter P and then the word "interest" and then ".com," and just like that my love of Pinterest was born. My pins at the time included things like paint chip DIYs, lots of braids and messy buns, banana ice cream, and many ridiculous quotes. Not long after this, I threw a *Cars* party for my little brother based on the movie, using tons of inspiration I had found on Pinterest. I hung a sign on the iced tea that said Unleaded Gas, and one for the blue raspberry punch that said Antifreeze. Not to mention several other obsessive details and decorations.

In college and even beyond, if a birthday or milestone needed to be celebrated, I would run into Target or Hobby Lobby and come out having spent at least fifty dollars on supplies for the latest "little party" I planned. Looking back, I can say now that often these parties were more for me than they were for the person I wanted to celebrate. I enjoyed creating beautiful cakes or pulling together a really cute theme so I could show off my creativity, and to be even more honest, I often created these beautiful parties with the thought of what the social media post would look like in the end.

Finding My Why

One significant shift happened when I started developing recipes to share online. At the time, I enjoyed the challenge of making an elaborate dessert, but when I started sharing recipes online, I found that people didn't want to spend a bunch of time or need to order specialty tools or ingredients to produce a beautiful and yummy dessert. I also realized very quickly that I needed a good "why" if I was going to keep sharing recipes online. There were thousands and thousands of recipes already being shared. Why should I be posting recipes? Over time, God clarified my why. It was people.

I knew that whenever I made dessert, it had the power to bless and encourage other people; I wanted to extend that impact. My new mission was to equip people with recipes that they could make to bless and help the people in their lives feel special. Yes, dessert is a simple thing, but I believed and still believe that this inspiration, as simple as it may be, can make a difference. When it came to recipe development, a new challenge was born. My goal was now to create easy-to-follow recipes that were delectable and also visually appealing. And I loved it! It was so exciting to see that people were making the recipes and blessing the people in *their* lives. My hope and prayer is that this book is a continuation of that mission and that more and more people are celebrated and encouraged through it.

Cutting Back

Another part that played into my view on celebrations and baking was my journey into minimalism. I wouldn't call myself a minimalist, but over the past five years I have worked hard to declutter and keep the junk from coming into my space. I found that whenever I hosted a themed party, I bought new decorations to match the theme. When the celebration ended, I either got rid of them and felt guilty, or hung on to them and felt frustrated by the clutter I now had to store. The same thing went for my baking projects. There was always a specialty mold, tool, or ingredient to buy, only to use it once and then let it sit dormant in my kitchen cupboard. My newfound more minimalist lifestyle and these themed parties and complex desserts did not play well together.

Maybe you can relate to this scenario and feel frustrated by all of your effort and waste. Or maybe you throw up your hands and say, "Katie, I cannot relate at all. I don't enjoy hosting celebrations. Going on Pinterest just overwhelms me, and I don't even know where to start with throwing a themed party." Or maybe you even allow busyness and overwhelm to keep you from celebrating at all. The good news is that celebrating doesn't have to be this way.

Returning to My Roots

My perspective on celebration shifted when I realized that the parties I hosted or attended weren't enjoyable or special because of the theme or the decorations or all the money I spent or the elaborate desserts. It was the simple things, like hosting a honey roast, playing a simple game, or making a handmade birthday banner.

The one thing that made everyone feel special was a simple but homemade dessert. The dessert represented forethought, time, and love. Thinking about what kind of dessert the person I was celebrating would like, planning ahead to get all of the ingredients, and spending time making the dessert shows that I care. Not to mention how sitting down together and eating has the power to pull people together. It dawned on me that a lot of the simple things that my family did growing up were game changers. This shift made life easier for me and made the person of honor feel special and loved—which was the whole point.

Recently I listened to a podcast where two ladies said that we live in a culture that celebrates way too much. They described their annoyance with being expected to get a gift for every little accomplishment, graduation, or event. I disagree with what they said, but I think I agree with what they meant.

I don't think Americans celebrate too often, but I do think we tend to celebrate too big. Celebrations can become huge catered gatherings with bounce houses and swag bags and a massive gift table. I am inviting you to something simpler: a gathering of people over dessert. Imagine people feeling connected and relaxed, while the guest of honor feels cherished and basks in this uncomplicated affair. Also, fun fact: I once read a study in which researchers found that receiving a gift was the very last thing on the list of what made people feel special.

Why Celebrate?

A few years ago, my friend Tammy shared this conversation, and it really stuck with me: Her brother asked how she and her family were doing and what their family had been up to. Her response started off with, "Busy..." Before she finished, her brother cut her off. "'Busy' is so boring. Everyone is busy!" he said.

The funny thing is that saying "busy" is often how I would answer this question too. Busyness can put time into double speed. At the end of it we often feel we have little to show for all that running around and stress. Celebration takes these busy stretches of life and punctuates them. Celebration adds meaning and purpose to our lives. In fact, celebration has been proven to improve optimism, increase creativity, build community, and even build resilience.

As a Jesus follower, I also view celebration through the lens of the Bible. Each person is created by God in His image and is intrinsically valuable and worth being celebrated. Through the gospel, each person's innate value is seen at a greater depth. God's love to us through Jesus compels us to love and encourage one another. Celebration, ultimately, points to the goodness of God and praises Him for His provision and work in the life of the person we celebrate. In the Old Testament we see celebrations of remembrance like the Passover, Feast of First Fruits, and Pentecost. These annual celebrations pointed to God's faithfulness and work throughout generations. They exemplify how we can punctuate the mundane and point to God.

10 Practical Steps to Celebrate More . . . Today!

Okay! Have I convinced you that celebrating more is doable? Good. You might wonder where to get started, so here is a rapid-fire way to get going ASAP. Momentum is a powerful thing. The point of this cookbook is not for you to become the "hostess with the mostest," but instead, it is simply an inspiration and invitation to celebrate more, and more meaningfully. The hardest part for me in starting something new is getting going. These ten steps are ways to dip your toe in the water and get started because often, once we start, we realize it's not hard and that it's actually enjoyable.

1. Make a list of the people or groups you want to be intentional about celebrating every year. Jot down any important dates if you know them, such as anniversaries, birthdays, and neighborhood block parties. Pop these dates on your calendar, whether it's hanging on your wall or in your phone.
2. On pages 15–21, I detail what I keep in my fridge, freezer, and pantry to be ready to celebrate. Keep your essentials on hand. If you have to run out every time you want to celebrate, you are less likely to commit to the event, and you will end up wasting money and time.
3. Start small when you plan out your next celebration. You don't have to invite everyone you know. Invite a few people over, choose a dessert, and write a little birthday or congratulatory card. It's really that simple. Give yourself an easy win!

4. Here's a list of freezer-friendly recipes that you can make and keep in the freezer so you're ready when a celebration pops up.

    - Chocolate Revel Bars, page 86
    - Speedy Chocolate Cake, page 132
    - Triple Layer Carrot Cake, page 34
    - Almond Croissant Blondies, page 157
    - Shortcut Chocolate Whoopie Pies, page 155
    - Daddy's Favorite Gingersnaps, page 80

5. Stay off Pinterest as you plan and prepare. I really do enjoy Pinterest, but it's easy to start to snowball and make a bigger, more complicated, and more expensive celebration.
6. Take action. Don't feel like you need to get through this entire book before you start celebrating. Try something today! Momentum is a powerful tool. If you don't have something big to celebrate, check out my chapter on celebrating the little things on page 127. Is there a small celebration you can have today?
7. Shift your mindset. Remember that the goal is not to impress your guests but to make the person of honor feel special and loved. So don't obsess about how clean your house is—we're not trying to make ourselves look good, but make others feel special.
8. Words are powerful. It can be such a game changer when we regularly express how we feel about someone. You can write down these feelings (see page 50 for how to write a meaningful birthday card) or speak them (see page 124 for how to host a honey roast). I believe that conveying your feelings for your people will change your life!
9. Celebration has the power to pull people together. Use it. Invite people intentionally, whether to create new bonds or build existing bonds.
10. Don't get hung up on tradition. Not every celebration will look the same year to year, and that's okay. One year, a birthday party may have a long guest list, and the following year, it may be just your immediate family. It's about celebrating more—not perfectly.

My Essential Tools

While I wouldn't call myself a full-blown minimalist, I do work to have a "more simplified" cabinet and pantry. Below are the basic tools and pans that I use and what you will need to make the recipes in this book.

Stand Mixer with Paddle and Whisk

The holy grail is most definitely the KitchenAid mixer. They last forever, and the high price tag is worth it when you consider the cost per use. Each recipe in this book will specify whether to use the paddle attachment or the whisk attachment. Use the paddle attachment to combine ingredients without incorporating air. The paddle is particularly good at smoothing out lumps. The whisk attachment is used to whip air and achieve lots of volume in ingredients like cream and egg whites. Make sure to always scrape down the sides and the bottom of your stand mixer bowl. You can use a hand mixer instead, but it is not quite as slick as a stand mixer.

Mixing Bowls (Small, Medium, and Large)

When I'm not using my stand mixer, I am using a bowl to whisk or cream my ingredients by hand. It is helpful to have a few bowls in a variety of sizes. I prefer glass mixing bowls, but metal or plastic work too.

Rubber Spatula

I am very picky about the rubber spatulas I buy. I prefer a spatula that is one solid piece, meaning that the top and handle are not two different materials but are instead molded together as one piece. They seem to wash up better and last longer.

Whisk

You get what you pay for when it comes to whisks. Cheaper whisks will come apart after a few washes. I have been singing the praises of the GIR whisks for years, and they continue to be a personal favorite.

Liquid Measuring Cups

If you've ever wondered why you need both liquid and dry measuring cups, the reason is if you fill a dry measuring cup all the way full with liquid, it's very hard to move without spilling. Liquid measuring cups allow you to fill to the exact line and easily pour the liquid where you need it with the spout. The classic liquid measuring cup size is the 2-cup, but I have found that a mini 2-tablespoon measuring cup allows me to measure small amounts of liquids like extracts precisely without making a mess. My nonessential favorites include the 5-ounce, 1-cup, and 4-cup measures. Buy a quality measuring cup—or even better, buy one with raised measurements, as cheap liquid measuring cups become hard to read as the numbers fade.

Dry Measuring Cups

Dry measuring cups are pretty straightforward. They typically come with a 1, ½, ⅓, and ¼-cup size. Some also have a ⅔ and ¾ cup. I prefer either plastic or metal cups.

Measuring Spoons

This probably sounds obvious, but make sure that your measuring spoons fit inside your spice jars. I prefer narrow measuring spoons as, even up to the tablespoon, they all fit inside the narrow spice jars I get from the grocery store.

Bench Scraper

This is a simple tool that can be used in myriad ways. I use my bench scraper to smooth out frosting on the sides of a layer cake, to cut bars, and to bring dough together or portion it into pieces.

Offset Spatula

An offset spatula works well for frosting a layer cake or making your no-bake cheesecake perfectly smooth on top. In a pinch, you can use a butter knife, but the beauty of an offset spatula is that it has a straight edge, and the bend in the spatula means that you have perfect control and your wrist stays out of the batter or frosting you are spreading.

Muffin Pan

I love a bargain as much as the next girl, but don't opt for the cheapest pan on the shelf. A high-quality pan conducts the heat evenly and helps your cupcakes and muffins bake properly. If you feel like your pan is worn out, you might be surprised by the difference an upgrade would make.

Square Baking Pan (9 × 9-Inch or 8 × 8-Inch)

Everyone should have a small basic pan that handles blondies, brownies, or whatever you throw in there. Again, good-quality aluminum pans make all the difference. The recipes in this book are developed using a 9-inch square pan, but if you have an 8-inch pan, know that it will produce a thicker cake that will take extra time to bake.

9 × 13-Inch Pan

I skip the glass and ceramic and prefer to bake in an aluminum pan. It's obviously one of the more common sizes of pans and is great in between your square pan and rimmed baking sheet.

Rimmed Sheet Pan (13 × 18-Inch)

I have so many of these aluminum baking sheets, also known as the "half sheet pans," and I don't regret it. They can be used to bake cookies, make roll cakes, build poke cake, and so much more! Check out chapter 9 to see an entire chapter dedicated to this versatile pan.

Round Cake Pans

Again, I prefer the aluminum version of these pans. There are many different sizes of round cake pans. The recipes in this book will strictly use 8-inch round pans. I recommend having two so you can quickly build layer cakes.

Loaf Pan

These recipes were tested using 8½ × 4½-inch aluminum loaf pans. Pay careful attention to the size of the loaf pan you use. If you use a 9 × 5-inch loaf pan, it is double the volume and bakes up much thinner and much quicker.

Immersion Blender

An immersion blender is handy because you can quickly blend anything, including hot compotes, without transferring them to your blender. It's a versatile little appliance to add to your collection. If you already have a full-size blender, they can be used interchangeably.

Paring Knife

Nothing too crazy here. I use a paring knife to hull and slice strawberries and other fruit. It also works well to cut puff pastry.

Bread Knife

A long serrated knife can level a cake, cut croissants, or cut a layer cake.

Fine Mesh Sieve

I use a sieve to strain out lumps in my lemon curd and sift powdered sugar over my coconut croissants.

Spring-Loaded Scoops (Large and Small)

I use a large scoop to portion out my cupcake batter, a smaller scoop to portion cookies, and an even smaller scoop to make truffles!

Plastic Wrap

I use plastic to wrap up cake layers to help keep them nice and moist, and it's just what you need to press to the surface of curd or custard to prevent a skin from forming. My favorite by far is the Glad Press'n Seal wrap.

Parchment Paper

You can easily find parchment paper in rolls, but I prefer ordering (13 × 18-inch) parchment sheets. They lay flat and fit perfectly onto rimmed baking sheets. Be sure to buy parchment paper and NOT waxed paper—these are two different things. Waxed paper cannot go in the oven.

Saucepan

A medium-size stainless-steel saucepan is a workhorse in the kitchen. While I love using my microwave to make curd, ganache, custard, and so much more, a saucepan on the stove can do everything a microwave can. I break this all down on page 23.

Piping Bags

While plastic zipper bags can get you by in a pinch, a piping bag will do the job much more effectively. Stay away from cheap bags, as they can burst mid-piping. My favorite type of bag is the disposable 16-inch piping bags from Wilton.

Piping Tips

The good news is that you don't need many tips to accomplish several different looks. I recommend a large star tip like the Wilton 1M or the Ateco 826, and a large round tip like the Wilton 2A.

Cupcake Liners

I have used both cheap and more spendy cupcake liners. This is another case of you get what you pay for. The parchment liners from PaperChef are by far the best. If you end up with cheaper paper liners, the cake can stick to them when you peel them back, spritzing the liners with a bit of nonstick cooking spray can help.

My Pantry Essentials

All-Purpose Flour

Flour gets compacted when it's packaged and shipped, so fluff up your flour with a large spoon before measuring. Also, be sure to use a spoon to scoop flour into your measuring cup instead of dipping your measuring cup into your flour, and use the flat side of a butter knife to level off the top.

Sugar

When a recipe calls for sugar, it refers to granulated sugar or castor sugar. There is no need for any special treatment when measuring.

Powdered Sugar

Just like flour, powdered sugar can get compacted, so give it a fluff and use a spoon to scoop it up. Sifting powdered sugar prevents lumps in your frosting. If you whip your frosting in a stand mixer with the whisk attachment, it should get the lumps out, but if you're mixing it by hand, run it through a sieve to break up any lumps.

Brown Sugar

All the recipes in this book have been developed with dark brown sugar. I prefer the deeper molasses flavor, but if you only have light brown sugar on hand, you can substitute it without any issue. Because brown sugar is moist, you must pack it into the measuring cup using another measuring cup or your fingers until it is full. Always store brown sugar in an airtight container. If you ever have an issue with it drying out and getting hard, put a slice of bread into your container overnight, and it should soften up by the next day.

Coconut

I prefer to use unsweetened coconut flakes in all of my baking. Using unsweetened coconut allows me to control the sweetness in my recipes. In the grocery store, you will often see both shredded coconut and coconut flakes, and either will work in these recipes. I love the look and texture of the big coconut flakes. I buy several bags of coconut flakes at a time from Bob's Red Mill. In my opinion, they have the corner on the unsweetened coconut flake market, if such a thing exists.

Unsweetened Cocoa Powder

Any recipe that calls for cocoa powder is referring to unsweetened cocoa powder, not hot cocoa powder mix. All of the recipes in this book are tested using natural cocoa, which is the most typical cocoa you'll find in the grocery store (think Hershey's cocoa powder) as opposed to Dutch-process cocoa that has been alkalized to reduce the acidity.

Nuts

I use a wide variety of nuts in my baking—some raw and some salted and roasted. Here's what I keep on hand: First, the raw nuts I use are pecans and sliced almonds. Then, for roasted nuts I keep pistachios, mixed nuts, and peanuts.

Sweetened Condensed Milk

Sweetened condensed milk should not be confused with evaporated milk. It is made by evaporating part of the water content and adding sugar, which results in a sweet, syrupy milk. I like to keep a can or two at the ready.

Dulce de Leche

Dulce de leche is another canned product similar to sweetened condensed milk, but it is caramelized, resulting in a (surprise, surprise) caramel-like product. You'll find it right next to the evaporated milk as well as the sweetened condensed milk on the grocery store shelf.

Chocolate Chips

The classic chocolate chip is the semisweet. Depending on your preference, you can opt to stock up on milk chocolate or bittersweet chips if that's more your thing. I also keep white chocolate chips on hand.

Baking Chocolate Bars

I keep a stash of bittersweet and white chocolate bars on hand. They can be chopped and added to cookies, melted and stirred into a frosting or batter, or turned into a pile of chocolate curls using a vegetable peeler.

Baking Mixes

I do make many treats from scratch, but I'm not above using a mix to speed up the process and simplify the ingredient deck. I rarely make a brownie from scratch and prefer the Ghirardelli brand. My favorite cake mixes are from Betty Crocker, with my top two being the Triple Chocolate and French Vanilla. I would give their lemon and spice mixes an honorable mention.

Graham Cracker Crumbs

I never make my own graham cracker crumbs, but instead, I always buy them crushed. Not only is it convenient, but I prefer the flavor, as they are more salty and have less cinnamon, which I like in my desserts. But feel free to crush up regular graham crackers in a plastic ziplock bag with a rolling pin or cast-iron pan. If you have a food processor, you can give them a whirl.

Oils

I typically use canola oil for all my baking, but vegetable oil can be easily swapped. Avocado oil is the next best choice if you are trying to stay away from seed oils. I am not too picky when choosing a brand of canola oil, but Chosen is my preferred brand for avocado oil. I use coconut oil to create a hard-shell chocolate.

Nonstick Cooking Spray

I prefer to use a regular cooking spray like Pam rather than baking spray, which is a combination of flour and oil. You can also use butter or oil, but I favor the spray for its convenience.

Peanut Butter

It's not the time to make healthy choices when picking up peanut butter for baking. Skip the natural kind of peanut butter that separates; instead, you want something that is stable like the traditional Jif or Skippy.

Leavener

Baking powder and soda are similar but are not the same. Do not use them interchangeably. Some recipes use just one or the other, and some use both. Make sure to replace them regularly if you are not using them up. Once open, they will last about six months to a year.

Salt

The recipes in this book were tested with regular table salt. In recipes where I finish with flaky salt, I use Maldon Sea Salt Flakes that I pick up at my local cooking store or on Amazon.

Spices and Extracts

Spices and extracts give you the power to majorly impact the flavor without any special fresh juices, pods, bark, or leaves. Vanilla is the obvious standard extract, but equally important to me is almond extract. I also keep coconut and lemon on hand. My top spices for baking are cinnamon, nutmeg, ginger, and pumpkin pie spice.

Instant Coffee

Instant coffee is the unsung hero of so many recipes. It injects robust coffee flavor and is a humble jar of granules that will keep in your pantry for up to two years. This is one area I don't see a need to splurge when used in dessert. I don't find that better quality makes a noticeable difference.

Almond Paste

This thick paste consists of ground almonds, sugar, and almond extract. It adds almond flavor and a moist, chewy texture to baked goods.

My Fridge Essentials

Butter

I break the cardinal baking rule and prefer to use salted butter. All of the recipes in this book are tested with salted butter. If you use unsalted butter, you may want to adjust the salt to compensate.

Cream Cheese

I always keep a block or two of cream cheese on hand, as it keeps for several months unopened in the fridge.

Mascarpone

Mascarpone is similar to cream cheese but has a higher percentage of fat, producing an extra creamy cheese. Cream cheese can be substituted for mascarpone, but it will be lacking a bit in flavor and creaminess.

Sour Cream and Greek Yogurt

I usually have these both on hand—one for tacos and the other for my morning apple yogurt bowls, but when baking, these two can be used interchangeably, so use what you have.

Heavy Whipping Cream

This ingredient is a miracle worker in many recipes. It transforms simple pantry ingredients into impressive desserts. While it keeps for up to a month unopened, once opened, it will last for five to seven days.

Eggs

All of the recipes in this book have been tested using large eggs, so to achieve consistent results, skip the extra-large and jumbo eggs in the grocery store. If you are using homegrown eggs, the size may vary, but just know that one large egg is three tablespoons of liquid.

Yeast

I prefer to work with active dry yeast, but if you only have instant yeast, feel free to substitute it. Yeast, once opened, can be stored in the fridge for up to four months and in the freezer for up to six months. If you're not sure if your yeast is still good, stir it in a bit of warm water and sugar and wait ten minutes. It should be fragrant and foamy; if not, it's no good.

My Freezer Essentials

Puff Pastry

This is a great staple to keep in your freezer so you're ready to transform simple ingredients into spectacular flaky treats.

Frozen Fruit

Fresh fruit is great, but it's best when enjoyed seasonally. Frozen fruit is not only a great way to save money but also super flavorful. My freezer usually has a variety of blueberries, raspberries, cherries, strawberries, peaches, and mangos.

Baking Basics

Prepare

Before making a new recipe, look through the ingredient list. Do you have everything? There's nothing worse than getting five ingredients into a bowl and then realizing that you are out of the next ingredient, and now you have to figure out what to do with everything in your bowl. Check the time. Do you have enough time to accomplish this recipe? Do you have to chill it before serving? Remember that the active time can vary. Some people may need more or less time. If you have little helpers, it may take longer. Read through the method. It will only take a minute or two, but it will increase your efficiency because you will understand where the recipe is headed. This will also clarify what pans or tools you need for the recipe.

I recommend pulling out all the ingredients you will need. Not only is this more efficient, as you will have everything in front of you as you start baking, but it will also be a final check that you do indeed have the necessary ingredients.

Keep It Clean

If you're going to bake, it is inevitable that you will also have dirty dishes. Some of you already have great habits when it comes to cleaning as you bake, and you could teach me a thing or two. But if you struggle in this area, it can start to take the fun out of baking when you wind up with piles of dishes. So, before you start baking, run a sink full of hot, soapy water, empty your dishwasher (if you're blessed to have one), and take your garbage out if it's full (or nearly full). While you are measuring, beating, stirring, and whisking, throw the dirty dishes into the soapy water.

As I add an ingredient, I will put each of them away. For example, I measure and dump the flour in. I snap the lid on the canister and put it away. This helps me prevent missing an ingredient and simultaneously clears off my counter. Once you put the dessert in the oven or fridge, immediately go to your sink and do the dishes. The "fresher" they are, the easier they are to clean. I do not always do this perfectly and have procrastinated a time or two (or two hundred), but it is a muscle, and the more you do it, the easier it is and the more you will enjoy baking.

Prep Your Pans

For a round cake pan or sheet pan, cut a piece of parchment that will fit into the bottom of the pan. Spray a bit of nonstick cooking spray on the pan and then place the parchment on top. This helps prevent the parchment paper from moving. Spray the bottom and sides with more nonstick cooking spray.

To remove the dessert, run a butter knife around the edge of the pan so that any bits that are stuck get loosened. Flip the pan upside down onto your work surface. Carefully remove the pan and peel off the parchment paper.

For a square or rectangle pan, measure and cut two pieces of parchment paper—one that will fit the length of the pan and come up the sides and hang over a few inches past, and one that will fit the width of the pan and also come up the sides with an overhang. If you use a square pan, these two pieces will be the same size. Spray a bit of nonstick cooking spray on the pan and then place one of the parchment sheets on top. Spray a bit more and place the second piece running the other direction. Spray the bottom and sides with more nonstick cooking spray.

To remove the dessert, simply pull up on the parchment paper overhang and lift the dessert out.

Know If It's Done

The times listed in these recipes are merely guidelines, so it is essential to check for the visual cues listed in each recipe. Ovens and microwaves vary greatly. Humidity and warmth in a kitchen will also affect the timing of whatever you are making.

Fill a Piping Bag

Snip a small corner off the piping bag about two-thirds the length of your piping tip. Fold the top of the bag back and out of the way. Drop your piping tip into your bag and push it to the end. If the hole is too small for the tip to fit in the end, snip off a bit more. Remember that you can always trim more off the bag, but if the hole gets too big, it is no good because the tip will fall out.

Place the tip of the piping bag down into

a large drinking glass. Fold the edges over the sides of the glass. Use your spatula to fill the bag. Fill it about one-half to two-thirds of the way full. If it gets too full, it is hard to control. Twist the open end and squeeze to apply pressure from the back of the bag until the filling comes out.

Microwave

As you get into these recipes, you'll quickly learn I love using my microwave for many things, especially when making curds and custards. You never have to worry about scorching the mixture or standing over your stove constantly stirring. You can start it and walk away until the time is up. It's important to note that microwaves vary significantly based on their wattage. Microwaves generally range from 600 to 1200 watts. The recipes in this book were tested with a 1200-watt microwave. The lower the wattage, the longer it will take. Using a low wattage microwave can cause times listed in recipes to double, so instead look for visual cues indicated by the recipes instead of going just based on time. The time listed is just a guideline.

As I've made very clear, I love using my microwave. However, I know that not everyone has a microwave or prefers to use one, so let's break down how to convert recipes from the microwave to the stovetop.

Melt Butter: This one's kind of obvious, but place the butter in a saucepan and heat on medium-low heat until melted, stirring occasionally. If you are making curd or penuche, make sure to allow the butter to cool slightly before moving on to add ingredients to the saucepan.

Melt Chocolate: Place a heatproof bowl over a medium saucepan with an inch of water simmering in it. The bowl should not touch the water. Place the chocolate in the bowl and stir until melted.

Make Custard: Heat the milk mixture in a saucepan over medium-low heat until steamy but not boiling. Slowly pour about a half cup of the hot milk into the egg yolk mixture, stirring constantly. This tempers the egg yolks. Pour the tempered egg yolks back into the saucepan with the rest of the milk, stirring while you pour it back in. Return to the burner over medium-low heat and stir frequently until it is thick (like the consistency of yogurt or pudding).

Make Curd: Heat the ingredients for a curd in a saucepan, stirring frequently over medium-low heat until slightly thickened. If you dip a spoon in the curd and run a finger across the back, it should leave a line and not flow back over it.

Whip Peaks

When whipping cream or egg whites, the three main stages are soft, medium, and stiff. The best way to check is stop the mixer, take the whisk attachment off, and flip it upside down.

Soft Peaks: The cream will fold over, and after about five seconds will fold back into itself.

Medium Peaks: The cream will be sturdy but fold over slightly at the tip.

Stiff Peaks: The egg whites will stand straight up without folding over.

Thick: If I am whipping ganache, cream cheese, or mascarpone, I will use the word "thick" to describe the desired texture. One way to check for this is to take the mixing bowl off the mixer and tip it on its side. Look at the edge of your bowl. If your frosting or filling is thin enough to slide around, keep whipping, but if it stays in place, you're good to go.

Make Ahead/Manage Timing

Many recipes become more doable when you split up the work over a few days. Anytime you make a multi-component dessert, I recommend making the components on day 1 and assembling the dessert on day 2. For example, if you are making Coconut Cream Cake (page 32), on day 1 you can bake the cake layers, wrap, and freeze them, and make the custard and refrigerate it. Then on day 2, finish the frosting and assemble the cake. I love making desserts over multiple days because you never have to wait for something to cool. It becomes effortless when you organize this way.

Unlike most savory dishes that need to be made right before serving, many of the recipes in this book can be ready and waiting the day before. This is ideal if you're hosting any type of celebration. You don't need to be running around your kitchen at the last minute. You can simply pull out your finished dessert right before serving.

Speed Things Up

I wish I could say that I am always prepared and get my dessert done the day before, but that would be a lie. So if I am running out of time and need to speed up the process of making dessert, there are a few things I do.

A general rule is to transfer whatever needs to cool from the hot pan or bowl to a clean room-temperature vessel. If you have cake layers that need to be cooled, let them cool for ten minutes in their pan so they don't break apart. Then, remove them from their pans that are holding the heat, place them on a baking sheet, and pop them into the freezer to speed up the cooling process.

The same can be done with custard, filling, ganache, or curd. Spread it in a thin layer on a rimmed baking sheet and throw it in the fridge or freezer. Cover custards and curds in plastic wrap, pressing it to the surface to prevent a skin from forming. The freezer will be faster, but keep an eye on it, as the edges may start to freeze, and that's not what we're looking for.

Time to Dish It Up

At my house, when it's finally time to serve the dessert, a few people will head to the kitchen, brew the coffee, grab the plates, dessert, and forks, and start dishing it up. We'll typically "take everyone's order" and ask each person if they want dessert (or which one if there are multiple) and if they want ice cream. Our tradition is that the guest of honor gets their dessert first, and then we serve the rest from oldest to youngest. We try to respect our elders, and I think this is a small way to do that. Kids often get served first at dinner, so it's nice for them to practice their patience when it comes to dessert.

Another way we will serve dessert if it is an easy-to-grab treat like a blondie or a cupcake is to simply put the platter of desserts in the middle of the table or, if we are in the living room, on the coffee table, and everyone can grab what looks good to them.

The two Wilken nonnegotiables to enjoy dessert are vanilla ice cream and good coffee.

Vanilla Ice Cream

One of the highlights for girls living on the prairie was the Schwan's man. He would roll into the yard in his big truck, and we girls would run to the house, "Mom! The Schwan's man is here!" He would hand my mom a catalog filled with TV dinners, frozen vegetables, frozen cookie dough, and, most importantly, ice cream. We girls would gather around my mom as she began to dictate her order. The Schwan's man would check his little handheld keypad to see if what my mom ordered was on the truck. Without fail, my mom would order a six-quart bucket of vanilla ice cream. I'm not exaggerating when I say we ate ice cream almost every single day in the summer and many days, even in the winter. So anytime we had birthday cake, apple crisp, or dessert of most any kind, it was paired with vanilla ice cream. "Generous portions," like my dad used to always say. Sadly, the company has been sold, their trucks don't run in our area anymore, and they changed their vanilla ice cream recipe. We have backed down a bit on daily ice cream consumption, but we still prefer to enjoy cake and cookies with vanilla ice cream.

Coffee

I very strongly believe that dessert is better with coffee. It's why so many of the pictures in this book have cups of coffee in them—that's the way we enjoy sweets in this family. The bitterness in coffee perfectly offsets the sugar and richness in any dessert. Coffee preference is so personal; there's a million ways to make it and a wide variety of coffee quality. Yes, we do drink it black, but no judgment if you like your coffee very pale. That's how my brother Josh enjoys it.

Meet the Cast

My family is such a massive part of my life, and their names pop up a lot in this book, so before we go any further, let's put the names to the faces.

Grandma and Grandad Wilken are my dad's parents, and I grew up in the house next door to them on the ranch. They started their marriage as a pair of country school teachers and eventually transitioned to full-time ranching on our now-home place. My grandma taught me how to read and fostered a love of being in the kitchen. When I was in college and beyond, I would often live at my grandad's for the summer. They have two kids: my dad and **Aunt Linda**.

Grandma Pearl and Papa are my mom's parents, and they lived in the eastern

part of South Dakota. My papa grew up on a farm and worked as a butcher most of his life. My grandma was a schoolteacher. Their visits to our house were a highlight of my younger years. Not only was it fun to see them, but they would always load up their vehicle with lots of treats—ham, Danishes, frozen waffles (this was our favorite), caramel puff corn, party mix, and cheese balls. They have three kids: my mom, **Aunt Lisa**, and **Uncle Wade** (Unc for short).

Dad and I are basically twins separated by about 30 years. We have the same sense of humor, the same struggles, and the same eyes. My dad knows how to make work fun—it's why I keep coming back to help on the ranch in the summer.

Mom essentially runs a call center at the house. She has five girls out of the house, and most of them call her every day, some multiple times a day. It's a wonder she gets anything done! She started her career as a debate teacher but found a higher calling in staying home and taking care of us. Just kidding, but seriously.

My older sister **Ann** is the typical eldest child. She's very responsible, extremely generous, a bit bossy, and she enjoys filling out paperwork, if that tells you anything. Then it's me. Next is my sister **Tricia**. She is known as the wild child of the family. She likes to have fun, and the most dangerous thing to tell her is that she's funny. She'll just keep hamming it up and getting crazier and crazier. Tricia's married to **Cody**, and they have two boys, **Jacob** and **Jack**. And then there's **Susan—**she's almost perfect. She's sweet, easy to get along with, and laughs at pretty much everyone's jokes. She is married to **Tayte** and is the only sibling who doesn't live in South Dakota. Not that we're bitter about that.

The next three siblings are so spread out that they really are like the three babies of the family. **Lindsey** brings the energy and does almost everything with a smile. She married the neighbor boy, **Teigan**. Their ranch is about an hour from ours, but in South Dakota, that's almost next-door neighbors. **Josh** was born a people person and, much to our brother-in-law's dismay, works tirelessly to create nicknames for everyone in our family. He's a hard worker and is a big help to my dad. **Seth** has always been my little baby from the moment we brought him home from the hospital. My nickname for him is Pookie Bear, but I'm worried that he will soon be too cool for it. He's very adventurous and is usually trying to keep up with me on roller coasters. When it comes to skiing, though, I have made it clear that I won't set foot on anything above a blue, no matter how much he works on me!

How to Use This Book

What you are reading right now is a people-centered cookbook. I can already hear you say, "People-centered? You do know that I don't just sit at home and eat the entire pan of brownies on my own, right? Aren't all cookbooks centered around making for other people?" Okay, I agree that we often share our cakes and cookies with others when we bake, but what we are doing here is a little different. This book contains ideas for celebrations and doable desserts, but you won't see any federal holidays. No St. Patrick's Day, Labor Day, Thanksgiving, or even Christmas. The focus is not on the party but on the people.

Each of the next eight chapters focus on celebrating particular people or relationships in your life: the birthday person, the one you love, the people who have made an impact on your life, someone who has hit a major milestone, little reasons to celebrate the people in your life, mornings together with your people, and those you want to build community with.

Even though I stripped down these celebrations to simplify them and keep them meaningful, I still wanted to develop sweets recipes using easy techniques, basic pans, and go-to tools. I've worked to create recipes that produce memorable desserts but that don't require an Amazon order to pick up specialty ingredients or gadgets.

At the end of each chapter, you will see a celebration practice or two. This is a focused idea on how to make the guest of honor feel special, ways to simplify the celebration process, or ideas to make your celebration more memorable. These practices have been intentionally shaped to be effortless to pull off, and keeping in the minimalistic spirit, they use very few or no supplies. Just as my "why" in developing these recipes is blessing people, I hope you have the same "why" as you make the recipes from this book.

H
BIR
D

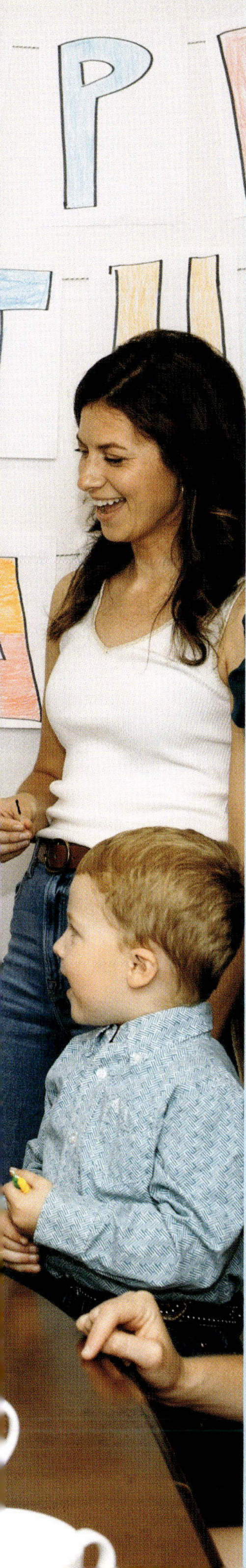

CHAPTER 2

Birthdays

[FUSS-FREE LAYER CAKES]

Over the last decade or so, I've been known as the "girl who makes the cupcakes." Despite the title, whenever I asked someone in my family what dessert they wanted for their birthday, they would almost always request some type of layer cake. There is something about layer cakes that makes them the iconic birthday dessert. But there are many pitfalls to look out for.

The cake can get stuck in the pan or break into chunks when you get it out. When you start stacking the layers, they might want to lean or tip over. And in my opinion, the most challenging step—actually frosting the cake! Getting the frosting smooth can be challenging and takes lots of practice, so I will show you techniques to disguise less-than-perfect results. All of the recipes in this chapter feature fuss-free ways to frost and finish each cake.

Birthdays are my favorite celebrations—and not just because of the delectable layer cakes, but because everyone has one each year, and there is nothing you can do to earn it. Each human is created by God and is worth being celebrated. Celebrating a birthday is really appreciating the fact that God made this amazing person and responding with gratitude to God for him or her. Growing up, birthdays have always been a part of our traditions, and not just for the kids in my family—adults too!

Black Forest Meringue Cake

This "cake" does not contain actual cake but two layers of crunchy, marshmallowy meringue. The sweet meringue contrasts with the bitter chocolate and tart cherries. I love the flavor of fresh raw bing cherries, but if this cake only had raw cherries, it would not stay together; it needs some "glue." This cake finds the best of both worlds by cooking half of the cherries into a sweet, thick compote and leaving the other half raw to preserve that fresh flavor.

ACTIVE TIME: 1 hour | **TOTAL TIME:** 2 hours 20 minutes | **YIELD:** 10–12 servings

INGREDIENTS

- Sit Back and Relax Meringue (page 217)
- 4 oz. bittersweet chocolate, divided
- 2 lbs. fresh bing cherries, pitted and halved, divided
- ⅓ cup sugar
- 6 tablespoons water, divided
- 2 tablespoons cornstarch
- Chocolate Whipped Cream (page 215)

DIRECTIONS

[1] Preheat the oven to 275 degrees.

[2] *First, make the meringue disks.* Prepare the Sit Back and Relax Meringue according to the recipe directions. Trace two six-inch circles onto a piece of parchment and place it writing-side down on a 13 × 18-inch rimmed baking sheet. Roughly chop 2 ounces of the bittersweet chocolate.

[3] Split the meringue in half and use an offset spatula to spread the meringue into two circles over the guides made on the parchment paper. Sprinkle the chopped chocolate over the top. Bake for 45 to 50 minutes or until the meringue changes from a glossy finish to a matte one. Turn the oven off and crack the door to let the meringue dry out for one more hour. Cool completely.

[4] *Next, make the cherry compote.* Add half of the cherries, sugar, and 2 tablespoons of water to a medium saucepan over medium heat. Allow the mixture to cook until the cherries begin to break down, about 10 to 15 minutes, stirring occasionally. Whisk ¼ cup water and cornstarch in a small bowl and pour it into the cooked cherries. Stir and cook until thickened, about 1 minute. Transfer to a storage container and refrigerate until chilled.

[5] *After that, make the whipped cream, chop the remaining chocolate, and finish the cherry filling.* Prepare the Chocolate Whipped Cream according to the recipe directions. Finely chop the remaining 2 ounces of chocolate. Mix the cooled cherry compote and the fresh cherries until they are coated with the compote.

[6] *Let's put it all together!* Place one meringue round on your serving dish. Use a large metal spatula and your hand to help move it. It may be a bit cracked, but that's totally okay. Spoon half of the chocolate whipped cream on and spread into an even layer. Spoon half the cherry mixture over the cream in an even layer. Place the second layer of meringue on top and repeat the chocolate whipped cream and the cherries. Sprinkle the finely chopped chocolate over the top. Cut into slices and serve. Store leftovers in the refrigerator.

Coconut Cream Cake

Coconut custard is one of my dessert staples, so I created a coconut cream frosting with a custard base. The recipe adds cooled custard to a sweetened creamed butter, producing a velvety, not-too-sweet icing. My favorite part about this cake is that the coconut flakes disguise any frosting mishaps. Truly, you can be pretty haphazard in your frosting application because it will all get covered up with coconut.

ACTIVE TIME: 50 minutes | **TOTAL TIME:** 1 hour 45 minutes | **YIELD:** 8–12 servings

INGREDIENTS

- Vanilla Doctored Cake Mix (page 214)
- 1 teaspoon coconut extract

Custard:

- 1 cup whole milk
- 6 tablespoons sugar, divided
- Pinch of salt
- 2¼ cups unsweetened coconut flakes, divided
- 2 egg yolks
- 1½ tablespoons cornstarch
- ½ tablespoon salted butter, softened
- 1 teaspoon vanilla extract
- 1 teaspoon coconut extract

Frosting:

- 1 cup salted butter, softened
- 1½ cups powdered sugar

DIRECTIONS

[1] Preheat the oven to 325 degrees. Grease and line two 8-inch round cake pans with parchment.

[2] *First, make the cake.* Prepare the Vanilla Doctored Cake Mix according to the recipe directions. Stir in 1 teaspoon coconut extract. Divide the batter equally between the two pans. Bake for 20 to 25 minutes or until the cake springs back when gently pressed. Cool completely. Run a butter knife around the edge of each cake to loosen it and remove from the pan. Wrap each layer in plastic wrap and freeze until ready to assemble.

[3] *Next, make the custard for the frosting.* Heat the milk, 3 tablespoons sugar, salt, and ¼ cup coconut in a microwave-safe dish until steamy (about 1 minute), but DO NOT boil.

[4] While milk mixture is heating, beat the remaining sugar, egg yolks, and cornstarch in a medium-size bowl until smooth.

[5] Slowly stream the hot milk into the yolk mixture, whisking constantly until it is smooth. This will slowly bring the egg yolks up to temperature.

[6] Microwave the custard for 1-minute intervals, stirring in between each interval, until thick, about 2 minutes. Add ½ tablespoon of butter, vanilla, and 1 teaspoon coconut extract. Stir until the butter has melted. Press a piece of plastic wrap to the surface of the custard. Refrigerate until completely chilled.

[7] *Now, make the frosting.* Cream 1 cup butter and the powdered sugar in a stand mixer fitted with a paddle attachment on medium-low speed until thick and fluffy. Add one spoonful of the cooled custard at a time, with the mixer running at low speed, until the custard is completely incorporated.

[8] *Assemble the cake.* Place one cake round on your desired serving platter. Spoon a generous half cup of frosting onto the cake and spread into an even layer using an offset spatula. Place the second cake layer on top and gently press so that it is level on top. Frost the sides and the top of the cake with frosting.

[9] Press the remaining 2 cups coconut flakes into the frosting. Using your hands, scoop up a handful of the coconut flakes and press them into the sides and top of the cake until the frosting is covered. Store in the refrigerator until ready to serve. Cut into slices and serve. Store leftovers in the fridge.

Tiramisu Icebox Cake

Tiramisu is such a fancy dessert despite being such a simple one to make, but I often struggle to find ladyfingers in my local grocery store. I swap the traditional ladyfingers for Milano cookies, which I seem to find everywhere, and I love the flavor and texture that the chocolate filling in the cookies adds to the dessert. Icebox cake is simply cookies and cream layered together and allowed to chill until the cookies soften. Make sure you give the cake at least 6 hours in the fridge; 8 is better! This gives the cookies time to soften and for the cream and the cookies to become one.

ACTIVE TIME: 25 minutes | **TOTAL TIME:** 8 hours 25 minutes | **YIELD:** 6–8 servings

INGREDIENTS

- 1 (8 oz.) pkg. mascarpone cheese
- ½ cup powdered sugar
- 1 teaspoon vanilla extract
- 1½ cups heavy whipping cream
- Cocoa powder for sifting (about 2 tablespoons)
- 2 (6 oz.) pkgs. milk chocolate Milano cookies
- ½ cup very strong coffee or espresso

DIRECTIONS

[1] *First, make the mascarpone cream.* In a stand mixer fitted with the whisk attachment, mix mascarpone, powdered sugar, and vanilla until smooth. Add the heavy cream and whip until medium peaks form.

[2] *Next, assemble the cake.* Create the cake base by spreading a half-inch thick layer of the cream in a 6-inch circle shape over your cake stand or plate. Sift a generous layer of cocoa over the cream.

[3] Dip both sides of each cookie into the coffee or espresso and place five soaked cookies in a single layer on top of the cream in an asterisk shape.

[4] Place about ⅓ cup of the cream over the cookies and spread evenly using an offset spatula.

[5] Repeat the layers—cocoa powder, soaked cookies, and cream—until you have used all the cookies. Stagger the cookies so they nestle into the two cookies below.

[6] Loosely cover with plastic wrap and refrigerate for 8 hours or overnight to allow the cookies to soften.

[7] Refrigerate until ready to serve. Before serving, top with more cocoa powder. Cut into slices and serve. Store leftovers in the refrigerator.

Triple Layer Carrot Cake

A traditional triple-layer carrot cake is typically baked in round pans, but for my fuss-free version, I bake the cake in one 13 × 18-inch rimmed baking sheet. Then, I just cut the cake into three equal pieces and layer them up. To keep things simple with frosting, I leave it as a naked cake. I use a piping bag to pipe dollops of frosting, so I never have to worry about getting crumbs in my frosting like I would if I were spreading the frosting on. Not only does this make the frosting process simple, but I also love the look of the layers of cake showing.

ACTIVE TIME: 55 minutes | **TOTAL TIME:** 1 hour 50 minutes | **YIELD:** 16–20 servings

INGREDIENTS

Cake:

- 1 cup sugar
- 1 cup dark brown sugar
- 1 cup canola oil
- ½ cup applesauce
- 4 large eggs
- 2 teaspoons vanilla extract
- 2 cups all-purpose flour
- 2 teaspoons baking soda
- 2 teaspoons baking powder
- 2 teaspoons cinnamon
- ½ teaspoon ground cloves
- ½ teaspoon ground ginger
- ½ teaspoon nutmeg
- ½ teaspoon salt
- 1 pound carrots, peeled and finely grated (about 3 cups)
- 1 cup chopped pecans

Frosting:

- ½ cup salted butter, softened
- 1 (8 oz.) pkg. cream cheese, softened
- 4 cups powdered sugar
- ¼ cup heavy whipping cream
- 2 teaspoons vanilla extract

DIRECTIONS

[1] Preheat the oven to 350 degrees.

[2] *First, make the cake.* Whisk the sugar, brown sugar, oil, applesauce, eggs, and vanilla in a medium-size mixing bowl. Add the flour, baking soda, baking powder, cinnamon, cloves, ginger, nutmeg, and salt. Stir until mostly combined.

[3] Add the carrots and pecans and stir until combined. Pour the batter into a greased and parchment-lined 13 × 18-inch rimmed baking sheet and bake for 20 to 25 minutes, or until the cake springs back when gently pressed. Allow it to cool. Loosen the edges of the cake from the pan using a butter knife to go around the outside.

[4] Place the cake in the freezer while you make the frosting. This makes the assembly process more manageable.

[5] *Next, make the frosting.* Cream the butter and cream cheese in a stand mixer fitted with a paddle attachment until smooth. Add powdered sugar one cup at a time, beating after each addition. Mix on low until incorporated, then increase the speed to medium-high and mix until fluffy and smooth, for about 30 seconds. Continue adding powdered sugar a cup at a time until you have incorporated all of it.

[6] Add the heavy cream and vanilla and beat on high speed until light and fluffy. Transfer to a piping bag fitted with a large round tip.

[7] *Now, let's put it all together.* Remove the cake from the freezer and invert the cake pan onto a clean counter. Lift the sheet pan off and carefully peel off the parchment paper.

[8] Trim about ½ inch of the cake off each side using a bread knife. This is an optional step, but it yields a cleaner final product.

[9] Cut the cake into 3 equal rectangles. You can eyeball 3 equal chunks or measure the length of the cake using a ruler now that you have cut off the edges. It should be about 16 inches long. If we divide 16 by 3, it is 5⅓ inches. Use a ruler to score the cake at the 5⅓-inch mark and repeat. Use a bread knife to make the final cuts to yield 3 equal pieces.

[10] Place one rectangle of cake on your serving board. Pipe dollops of cream cheese frosting in rows over the layer. Add another rectangle of cake on top. Gently press down on the cake layer. Repeat two more times. Refrigerate until ready to serve. Cut into slices. Store leftovers in the refrigerator.

Pistachio Crunch Cake

I love a dessert with some texture, and this one delivers! Baking the puff pastry circles between two baking sheets keeps them from puffing up, and instead, the layers bake up nice and crispy. Chocolate and chopped pistachios pile on even more crunch, and the pistachio cream pulls it all together for an addictive combination! I remember bringing this dessert home to the ranch one Friday night after a week of teaching, and my family started cutting little pieces off and snacking on them as we talked around the kitchen island. They kept cutting off little chunks, and before long, it was gone! That crunch does make it so addictive.

ACTIVE TIME: 1 hour | **TOTAL TIME:** 1 hour 25 minutes | **YIELD:** 6–8 servings

INGREDIENTS

- 1 sheet puff pastry (½ of a 17.3 oz pkg.), thawed
- 1 cup semisweet chocolate chips
- 1 tablespoon coconut oil
- ⅓ cup roasted salted pistachios, chopped, divided
- 1 (3 oz.) pkg. instant pistachio pudding
- 2 cups heavy whipping cream

DIRECTIONS

[1] *First, make the pastry layers.* Preheat the oven to 400 degrees. Roll the puff pastry sheet on a lightly floured surface until it is a 12 × 12-inch square. Use a small plate or cake pan as a guide to cut four six-inch circles; it will be a tight fit to get all four, so go all the way to the edge. Place on a parchment-lined 13 × 18-inch baking sheet. Poke each pastry circle several times with a fork to prevent bubbles or puffing. Place another piece of parchment paper and then another 13 × 18-inch baking sheet on top of the pastry. Bake for 17 to 20 minutes or until golden and crispy. Allow pastry to cool.

[2] Place chocolate chips and coconut oil in a small microwave-safe dish. Heat in the microwave for 30 seconds. Remove and stir. Continue heating for 15-second intervals, stirring between each interval until the chocolate is completely melted.

[3] Using an offset spatula, thinly spread chocolate over each piece of puff pastry. Set aside 1 tablespoon chopped pistachios for the top of the cake, and immediately sprinkle the remaining nuts evenly over the wet chocolate. Pop the tray of chocolate-covered pastry circles in the freezer for a few minutes or until the chocolate is firm.

[4] *Next, make the pistachio cream.* In a stand mixer, whip pudding mix and whipping cream together until stiff. The pudding will activate and quickly thicken up the cream as you are whipping. Transfer mixture to a piping bag fitted with a large round tip.

[5] Place one baked pastry circle in the center of a cake stand or plate. Pipe dollops of the pistachio pudding cream on top. Place another pastry circle on top and gently press down. Continue to layer pastry and cream. Finish by piping a pistachio pudding cream ring and sprinkle with the remaining chopped pistachios. Cut into wedges and serve. It is best enjoyed the day of. Store leftovers in the refrigerator.

Coconut Almond Crepe Cake

This impressive cake features several alternating thin layers of crepe and custard. The duo of coconut and almond appears in the custard, and the toasted sliced almonds and coconut flakes on top. To simplify this cake, prepare the coconut custard and the crepes the day before to avoid having to wait for everything to cool before assembly.

ACTIVE TIME: 1 hour 20 minutes | **TOTAL TIME:** 5 hours 15 minutes | **YIELD:** 8 servings

INGREDIENTS

- Coconut Cream (page 213)
- 1½ teaspoons almond extract
- Crepes (page 218)
- 2 tablespoons sliced almonds
- 2 tablespoons unsweetened shredded coconut
- 1 cup heavy whipping cream
- ¼ cup powdered sugar
- 1 teaspoon vanilla extract

DIRECTIONS

[1] Prepare the Coconut Cream according to the recipe directions. Stir in the almond extract. Refrigerate until chilled.

[2] Prepare the Crepes according to the recipe directions. Refrigerate the crepes until they are chilled.

[3] *Next, toast the almonds and coconut.* Once the last crepe has been removed from the pan, using the same skillet still set to medium-high heat, add the sliced almonds and shredded coconut. Stir frequently for 2 to 3 minutes until fragrant and lightly toasted. Turn the heat off and transfer the toasted almonds and coconut to a small bowl. Set aside to cool.

[4] *Let's make the filling now.* In a stand mixer, whip the heavy cream, powdered sugar, and vanilla until stiff peaks form. Reserve about ⅔ cup of the whipped cream and set aside.

[5] Add the rest of the whipped cream to the coconut cream and gently fold until no streaks can be seen and it is completely incorporated.

[6] *Time to put it all together!* Place a crepe in the center of a cake stand or plate. Top with about ¼ cup of the whipped coconut cream filling. Spread to the edge of the crepe using an offset spatula.

[7] Continue layering crepes and the whipped custard filling.

[8] Top with the reserved whipped cream and sprinkle with the toasted almonds and coconut.

[9] For clean-cut slices, refrigerate for at least 2 hours to allow the cream to set. Refrigerate until ready to serve. Cut into slices and serve. Store leftovers in the refrigerator.

Strawberry Coconut Cake

Growing up, Strawberry Coconut Cake was the cake that Grandma Wilken always made for my mom and aunt's birthday (these two sisters-in-law just happen to share the same day). It was always such a treat with strawberries, pecans, and coconut all making an appearance in the cake as well as the frosting. The textured frosting gives it a unique undone look, and any pink crumbs that wind up in the pink frosting are undetectable, making the frosting process very forgiving. My family serves this cake with giant scoops of vanilla ice cream.

ACTIVE TIME: 40 minutes | **TOTAL TIME:** 1 hour 40 minutes | **YIELD:** 8–12 servings

INGREDIENTS

Cake:

- ½ cup canola oil
- ½ cup whole milk
- 4 large eggs
- 1 (15.25 oz.) pkg. white cake mix
- 1 (3 oz.) pkg. strawberry gelatin
- 1 cup thawed and chopped frozen strawberries
- 1 cup unsweetened shredded coconut
- 1 cup chopped pecans

Frosting:

- ½ cup salted butter, softened
- 3¼ cups powdered sugar
- ½ cup thawed and chopped frozen strawberries
- ½ cup sweetened shredded coconut
- ½ cup chopped pecans

DIRECTIONS

[1] Preheat the oven to 350 degrees. Grease and line two 8-inch round cake pans with parchment.

[2] *First, make the cake layers.* Mix the oil, milk, eggs, cake mix, and gelatin in a stand mixer fitted with a paddle attachment until smooth. Add the strawberries, coconut, and pecans. Stir until combined.

[3] Divide the batter equally between the two pans. Bake for 18 to 22 minutes or until a toothpick comes out clean. Cool completely. Run a butter knife along the edge of the pan and remove each cake layer. Pop the cake layers in the freezer until you are ready to assemble.

[4] *Next, make the frosting.* Cream the butter and powdered sugar in a stand mixer fitted with a paddle attachment. Add the strawberries, coconut, and pecans and stir until incorporated.

[5] Place one cake round in the center of a cake stand or plate. Using an offset spatula, spread about ½ cup of the frosting evenly over the top of the cake. Place second cake round on top.

[6] Again, using the offset spatula, spread the frosting over the sides of the cake.

[7] Use a rubber spatula to plop the rest of the frosting on top of the cake. Spread evenly using the offset spatula.

[8] Refrigerate until ready to serve. Cut into slices and serve. Store leftovers in the refrigerator.

Chocolate Raspberry Waffle Cake

Feel like making a cake that doesn't require an oven? I've got you covered. Use your waffle iron for more than just breakfast with this drool-worthy waffle cake. The nooks and crannies of the waffles hold a rich ganache, balanced with the light chocolate whipped frosting and tart raspberry filling.

ACTIVE TIME: 1 hour 5 minutes | **TOTAL TIME:** 2 hours 35 minutes | **YIELD:** 8–10 servings

INGREDIENTS

- ½ cup Two-Ingredient Raspberry Filling (page 213)

Ganache:

- 1 cup semisweet chocolate chips
- ½ cup heavy whipping cream

Cake:

- 1 cup water
- ½ cup canola oil
- 3 large eggs
- ½ cup sour cream
- 1 (13.25 oz.) pkg. chocolate cake mix
- Chocolate Whipped Cream (page 215)
- 1 cup fresh raspberries, plus more for serving

DIRECTIONS

[1] *First, make the raspberry and ganache filling.* Prepare the Two-Ingredient Raspberry Filling according to the recipe directions. Refrigerate until chilled.

[2] Microwave the chocolate chips and heavy cream in a microwave-safe dish for 30 seconds. Stir. Microwave for 15 seconds more and stir. Repeat until no lumps remain. Allow to cool to room temperature.

[3] *Next, make the waffle cake layers.* Whisk the water, oil, eggs, and sour cream until combined. Add the chocolate cake mix and whisk until smooth.

[4] Heat an 8-inch round waffle iron. Spray with nonstick cooking spray. Pour about ⅔ cup chocolate cake batter into the center of the waffle iron. Cook until done, about 2 minutes, depending on your waffle iron. Carefully remove and place on a baking sheet. It's okay if some waffle triangles break apart; the frosting will hold them together as you assemble the cake. Continue cooking waffles, spraying the iron between each waffle until all of the batter is used. Cool completely. (You will have some extra waffles, so freeze them or enjoy a sweet breakfast tomorrow morning!)

[5] *Then make the frosting.* Prepare the Chocolate Whipped Cream according to the recipe directions, and transfer it to a piping bag fitted with a large star tip.

[6] *Let's pull it all together!* Place a waffle in the center of a cake stand or plate. Use a butter knife to spread about 3 tablespoons of ganache on top, gently pressing it into the nooks and crannies.

[7] Pipe dollops of whipped cream over the entire waffle. Drizzle about 1 tablespoon of raspberry filling over the frosting.

[8] Place another waffle on top. Gently press down and make sure the waffle is level.

[9] Repeat the process: ganache, whipped cream, raspberry filling, and another waffle until your cake is about 5 to 6 inches tall.

[10] Finish the cake by piping swirls of whipped cream over the top and placing fresh raspberries in the center.

[11] Refrigerate until ready to serve. Store leftovers in the refrigerator.

Parent Trap Ice Cream Cake

As '90s girls, my sisters and I were massive fans of Hallie and Annie in the movie The Parent Trap. *On the day the girls figure out that they are twins, they also realize that they are both fans of the combination of Oreo and peanut butter. These girls were really onto something. The combination works beautifully in this ice cream cake. You really can't go wrong with this cake and its layers of brownie, chocolate ganache, creamy peanut butter, and lots of Oreos.*

ACTIVE TIME: 30 minutes | **TOTAL TIME:** 9 hours 30 minutes | **YIELD:** 8–12 servings

INGREDIENTS

- ½ cup milk chocolate chips
- ⅓ cup heavy whipping cream
- 1 (18 oz.) pkg. brownie mix (and ingredients called for according to package directions)
- 1½ cups creamy peanut butter, divided
- 6 cups vanilla ice cream, softened
- 2 cups chopped Oreos (about 16 Oreos), divided

DIRECTIONS

[1] *First, prep the ganache.* Microwave the chocolate chips and heavy cream for 30 seconds. Stir. If any lumps remain, microwave for another 30 seconds and stir again. Allow to cool to room temperature.

[2] *Then, bake the brownie.* Cut a piece of parchment to fit in the bottom of an 8-inch round cake pan. Tear a long sheet of parchment about 30 inches long and fold it in half lengthwise. Place the parchment in the pan, overlapping the ends to form a collar that will hold not only the brownie but also the ice cream. You might have to wrestle with the parchment to get it to curve with the edge of the pan. Spray the bottom and about an inch up the side with nonstick cooking spray.

[3] Prepare the brownie mix according to the package directions and pour it into the prepared cake pan. Bake according to the package directions. Cool completely.

[4] *Time to put it all together!* Place peanut butter in a microwave-safe dish and heat for 15 seconds in the microwave to make it pourable. Stir. Set it aside.

[5] In a large mixing bowl, mix ice cream, ½ cup peanut butter, and ⅔ cup Oreos until the peanut butter and Oreos are swirled throughout. Do not overmix.

[6] Dump half of the ice cream mixture onto the brownie and use a spatula to pack down the ice cream to remove any air pockets. Spread the ganache, then ½ cup peanut butter, and sprinkle with ⅔ cup Oreos.

[7] Add the other half of the ice cream, spreading and packing until it is smooth. Top with the remaining ½ cup peanut butter and ⅔ cup Oreos. Place cake in the freezer.

[8] Freeze for at least 8 hours or overnight. Remove from the freezer 10 minutes before serving to allow the cake to soften slightly. Cut into wedges and serve. Store leftovers in the freezer.

Mocha Silk Pie Cake

I have made Mocha Silk Pie for years and my family loves it. The only thing to be aware of is that the classic French Silk Pie recipe uses raw eggs, which I have used for many years. Before serving it, I let everyone know that the pie contains raw eggs. My little brother Josh always refused to eat it. One time I gave him a hard time and he responded by saying, "I'm not going to eat rotten eggs!" All along, he thought I was warning against rotten eggs instead of raw eggs. The good news is you don't have to worry about either in this cake! The frosting mimics the mocha pie filling without using any eggs and instead relies on melted bittersweet chocolate and cream cheese to bring the richness. The cake layers are baked with a graham cracker crust to get that crispy, salty flavor to balance this overall sweet dessert.

ACTIVE TIME: 50 minutes | **TOTAL TIME:** 1 hour 50 minutes | **YIELD:** 8–12 servings

INGREDIENTS

Cake:

- 1½ cups graham cracker crumbs
- ⅓ cup butter
- Pinch of salt
- 1 cup water
- ½ cup sour cream
- ½ cup canola oil
- 3 large eggs
- 1 teaspoon instant coffee
- 1 (13.25 oz.) pkg. chocolate cake mix

Frosting:

- 4 oz. bittersweet chocolate, chopped
- 1½ cups + 1 tablespoon heavy whipping cream, divided
- 1 tablespoon instant coffee
- 1 (8 oz.) pkg. cream cheese, softened
- 2 cups powdered sugar
- 2 tablespoons cocoa powder

Chocolate Curls:

- 3 oz. bittersweet chocolate bar

Whipped Cream:

- 1 cup heavy whipping cream
- ½ cup powdered sugar
- 1 teaspoon vanilla extract

DIRECTIONS

[1] Preheat the oven to 350 degrees.

[2] *First, make the cake layers.* Toss the graham cracker crumbs, butter, and salt. Divide the buttered crumbs between two greased, parchment-lined 8-inch round pans. Use a spatula to press the crumbs into an even layer.

[3] Whisk the water, sour cream, oil, eggs, and instant coffee until combined. Add the cake mix and whisk until completely smooth. Divide the batter between the two pans and pour it over the prepared crust. Bake for 25 to 30 minutes or until the cake springs back when gently pressed. Cool completely. Pop the cake in the freezer while you make the frosting.

[4] *Next, make the frosting and assemble the cake.* Microwave the chocolate for 15-second intervals, stirring between each one until the chocolate is melted. Allow to cool.

[5] To make the coffee concentrate, microwave a tablespoon of heavy cream until warm, about 8 seconds. It doesn't take long. Add the instant coffee and stir until dissolved.

[6] In a stand mixer fitted with the paddle attachment, beat the coffee concentrate, cooled chocolate, cream cheese, powdered sugar, cocoa powder, and about ½ cup heavy cream until smooth and no lumps remain. Add the remaining cream and beat until smooth. Swap the paddle attachment for the whisk attachment and whip until thick, scraping the bowl occasionally.

[7] Place one cake layer graham cracker side down on your desired cake stand or platter. Dollop about ⅔ cup frosting on top of the cake. Use an offset spatula to spread it into an even layer. Place the next cake layer again graham cracker side down. Frost the sides and top of the cake generously. Place in the refrigerator while you make your chocolate curls.

[8] *Finish the cake with chocolate curls and whipped cream.* Firmly swipe a vegetable peeler across the bar of bittersweet chocolate to create curls. Place a rimmed baking sheet on your work surface to catch all the curls. Continue "peeling" until all of the chocolate has been broken down.

[9] Clear a spot in the middle of the sheet so that you can place the cake stand on the sheet of chocolate curls. Use your hand to pick up a generous scoop of curls and press them into the sides of the cake until the entire cake is covered in curls. Any curls that don't stick should fall back onto the baking sheet. You will want to work quickly so that the warmth of your hands doesn't melt the chocolate.

[10] In a stand mixer fitted with the whisk attachment, whip the 1 cup heavy cream, powdered sugar, and vanilla until medium peaks form. Transfer the cream to a piping bag fitted with a large star tip. Pipe swirls of frosting on top of the cake. Cut into slices and serve. Store leftovers in the refrigerator.

Cake Batter Ice Cream Cake

This clever recipe uses part of a cake mix to make a blondie base and the rest to make cake batter–flavored ice cream. Because cake mixes have raw flour, you must bake the dry cake mix before adding it to the ice cream. This ice cream cake has no lack of rainbow sprinkles, as they show up in the blondie base, no-churn ice cream, and all over the outside of the cake. Serious sweet tooths only past this point! If you are not prepared for a sugar rush—turn back now!

ACTIVE TIME: 1 hour | **TOTAL TIME:** 10 hours 10 minutes | **YIELD:** 8–12 slices

INGREDIENTS

Blondie:

- 1 (13.25) oz. pkg. yellow cake mix, divided
- ¼ cup salted butter, melted
- 1 large egg
- ¾ cup rainbow sprinkles, divided
- ¼ cup white chocolate chips

Ice Cream:

- 2 cups heavy whipping cream
- 1 (14 oz.) can sweetened condensed milk
- 1 tablespoon vanilla extract

Whipped Cream:

- 2 cups powdered sugar
- 2 cups heavy whipping cream
- 1 teaspoon vanilla extract

DIRECTIONS

[1] Preheat the oven to 350 degrees.

[2] *Heat treat part of the cake mix.* Measure 1 cup of the dry yellow cake mix onto a parchment-lined baking sheet. Bake for 3 to 5 minutes or until it reaches 160 degrees. This process heats the cake mix and kills any bacteria, as it does contain raw flour. Do not allow the cake mix to brown. Allow it to cool.

[3] *Next, make the blondie.* Cut a piece of parchment to fit in the bottom of an 8-inch round cake pan. Tear a long sheet of parchment about 30 inches long and fold it in half lengthwise. Place the parchment in the pan, overlapping the ends to form a collar that will hold not only the blondie but also the ice cream. You might have to wrestle with parchment to get it to curve with the edge of the pan. Spray the bottom and about one inch up the side with nonstick cooking spray.

[4] Mix the remaining cake mix (about 1½ cups), butter, and egg until smooth. Add ¼ cup sprinkles and white chips and stir until combined. Press into the prepared pan. Bake for 15 to 20 minutes or until golden brown and set. Allow it to cool.

[5] *Then make the ice cream.* In a stand mixer fitted with the whisk attachment, whip heavy cream until medium peaks form. Add the sweetened condensed milk, dry baked cake mix, and vanilla and whip until combined. Add ¼ cup of sprinkles and stir in using a spatula. Spread the ice cream in an even layer over the cooled cake base. Freeze for 8 hours or overnight.

[6] *Now, let's put it all together.* Fold the parchment collar down over the cake and flip the cake pan upside down. Pull the cake pan off and peel the parchment circle off the bottom. Flip the cake back over and place it on your desired cake plate. Peel the parchment pieces off the sides. Place in the freezer until you are ready to frost.

[7] In a stand mixer fitted with the whisk attachment, whip the powdered sugar with the remaining heavy cream and vanilla until medium peaks form. Reserve about ¾ cup whipped cream and set aside. Spread the remaining whipped cream over the sides and top of the cake using an offset spatula. Use your hand to press about 3 tablespoons of sprinkles around the bottom of the cake. Place the cake in the freezer for 15 to 20 minutes. While the cake gets a chance to firm up in the freezer, transfer the reserved whipped cream into a piping bag. Pipe swirls of whipped cream over the cake. Finish with the remaining sprinkles. Place in the freezer until ready to serve. Cut into slices and serve. Store leftovers in the freezer.

Write a Meaningful Birthday Card

When I was in high school, if I saw one of my friends heading toward me with a yearbook and a pen, I would duck for cover. I never knew what to write and often struggled to write something meaningful. It's not that I didn't like the person or they hadn't significantly impacted my life, but I struggled to express myself in short order. It might sound like I just need a therapist, but when I shared about my struggle online, I had many people admit they struggled with the same thing.

When it comes to birthday cards, I often procrastinate because I'm not sure what to say and then often don't even write the card because I have waited so long. So, let's knock it out together. My breakthrough came when I had received a few cards from a former boss. I kept thinking, "They write the most meaningful cards," but as I looked at them more closely, I realized they were typically not very long but followed a formula.

1. **Grab a card. Any card!** It doesn't have to be a birthday card. I prefer blank note cards because they're cheap and you can always have them on hand for any type of celebration.
2. **Start with addressing them.** This is kind of a no-brainer.

   Hey, Tricia!

3. **You're then going to open with some sort of introductory sentence like...**

   Happy birthday, sweet friend! I am so excited to celebrate with you today!

   OR

   It's your big day! I am so thankful we get to do life together.

4. **This is where the magic happens.** You're going to start off the next sentence with, "I so appreciate your..." You're then going to choose three things you appreciate, but you must be super specific! That's what makes it meaningful. For example:

   I so appreciate your quick wit, patience, and your excellent taste in coffee.

I really want this to be as helpful as possible, so I created a list of ideas to get you started:

Hilarious commentary	Kindness	Loving spirit	Persistence	Honesty
Behind-the-scenes work	Patience	Determination	Sense of humor	Creativity
Willingness to help	Bravery	Enthusiasm	Listening skills	Diligence
Considerate heart	Help	Excitement	Encouragement	Work ethic
Adventurous spirit	Courage	Classy style	Trustworthiness	Sincerity
Consistency in ____	Passion	Generosity	Laid-back attitude	Imagination

5. **If there is anything you want to add,** go for it—otherwise, wrap it up with a closing sentence.

Grateful for your friendship and can't wait to see what the next year holds!

6. **Sign off (and then do a victory dance!).** You just wrote a meaningful, personalized birthday card in no time.

Love you lots! ~Katie

Simple Birthday Decor

There are two types of people in this world: people who like to decorate for birthday parties and those who don't. Most people fall in the latter category, but the real question is, "Does decorating for a birthday party make it more meaningful?" Adding meaning and making people feel special is supposed to be the main purpose. But I think we can get sucked into Pinterest and think about posting pictures of the party decorations on social media more than we think of the impact we can make on the person we are trying to celebrate.

So...should we not decorate at all, then? Time out. If you enjoy decorating for birthdays, I am not telling you to stop but am simply encouraging you to evaluate the purpose behind what you're doing. Time in! Again, my goal is to make the celebration as meaningful as possible for the birthday person, so here are few ideas that I have found to work well:

1. **Create a handmade birthday banner.** Growing up, we would grab printer paper, someone would draw the block letters for the sign, and we kids would color them in. We'd run and grab a piece of dark orange baling twine from the Quonset, tape the papers on, and hang it up. Try to use supplies that you already have hanging around the house!
2. **If we can't find something** to string the banner up, we'll simply tape the papers on the inside of a window or door near where we come in.
3. **Keep decor super simple** by popping some sticky notes up on their bathroom mirror wishing them a happy birthday!
4. **If you're not into making a birthday banner,** invest in a reusable birthday banner that you can pull out again and again.

I know, for some people, handmade signs might seem chintzy, but I see them as extra special: You're not simply dropping money on some decorations at Target and throwing them up but actually taking the time and putting the thought into creating something special for the celebration.

What about themed plates and napkins? Or some balloons? Maybe some centerpieces? I challenge you to look around and use what you have! If you're in the habit of hopping on Amazon or heading to the store to grab some decorations before every party, this might feel strange, but push through it! Think about what you have on hand. Do you have a nice tablecloth? Throw it over your table! Fancier dishware? Put it out! Chalkboard or dry erase board? Design a birthday sign with a special message or maybe an acrostic using their name with words to describe them. For example: Josh: Jolly, Outstanding, Smart, Handsome. You get the idea. This might seem like something just for kids' birthdays, but I think these touches are still worth doing for adults. The people we are celebrating are important no matter their age, and while their reaction might not be as enthusiastic as an eight-year-old's, they are still blessed by these simple touches.

There are obviously more ideas you can come up with, but remember we are going for two things: *meaningful* and *simple*! It's got to check both boxes to work for me.

My Birthday Nonnegotiables

Life can be just plain nuts, and birthday celebrations can look so different from year to year. Sometimes a celebration might be well thought out and other times it might be more thrown together, but no matter what, I have a list of nonnegotiables that we do for every birthday.

1. We have a dessert (even if it's store bought).
2. We sing "Happy Birthday."
3. The celebration is captured in a picture.

Your list of nonnegotiables might be different from mine, but having a simplified checklist can reduce the overwhelm of birthdays. Just remember to make the birthday person feel special and loved!

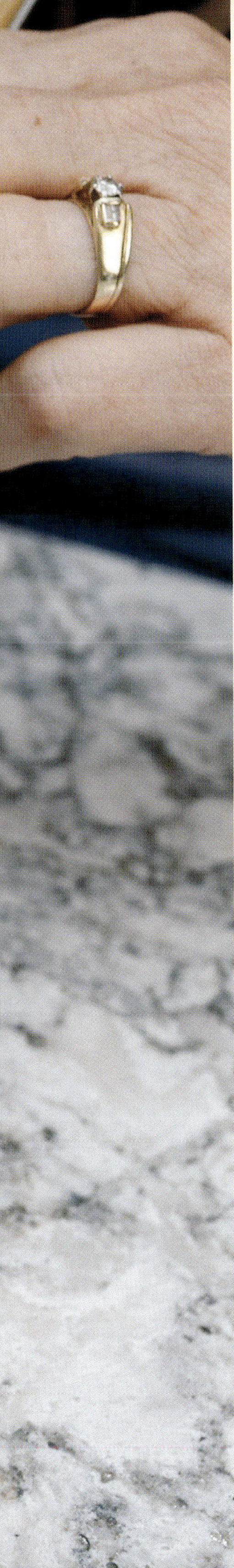

CHAPTER 3

Love

[DESSERTS FOR TWO]

Let's just point out the elephant in the room: You are reading a chapter about celebrating love written by a single girl. I see the irony, and I could put all sorts of disclaimers like, "You can make this for anyone you love. It doesn't have to be a significant other." And that's true. You can make these recipes for any two people you want. But I really did want this chapter to celebrate "romantic love," and the desserts in this chapter fit that theme.

Marriage is a beautiful gift from God. It's a picture of His relationship with us. Love itself is a gift from God and is worth being celebrated. Like my aunt Linda told my sister Ann—*in front of our entire extended family*—after Ann started dating her first boyfriend, "Love is a beautiful thing." (I think they broke up a few weeks later.)

When I'm making dessert for two people, I'm not looking for a fussy recipe that requires lots of steps and time. Instead, I prefer a recipe that comes together quickly. Bonus points if it's good to make ahead of time and keep in the fridge until you're ready to eat.

Cherry Almond Crumble

I have never been known for my "healthy recipes" and probably never will be—which is fine with me—but this recipe is probably the closest I'll ever get. This Cherry Almond Crumble starts with frozen sweet cherries, which don't get sweetened at all! While the crumble has a bit of brown sugar, this simple dessert lets the yummy fruit flavor shine! Because I am such a fanatic for almond extract, I had to put some almond extract in the whipped cream, as cherries and almond flavoring are a match made in heaven! If you're not as crazy about almond extract as I am, swap it for vanilla extract. Did I mention this recipe only takes 12 minutes to bake? If you're not adding frozen cherries to your grocery pickup order right now, what are you doing?

ACTIVE TIME: 15 minutes | **TOTAL TIME:** 30 minutes | **YIELD:** 2 servings

INGREDIENTS

- 1½ cups frozen sweet cherries, halved

Crumble:

- 3 tablespoons salted butter, melted
- ¼ cup old-fashioned oatmeal
- ¼ cup all-purpose flour
- ¼ cup light brown sugar
- Pinch of salt
- ¼ cup sliced almonds

Cream:

- ½ cup heavy whipping cream
- 2 tablespoons powdered sugar
- ¼ teaspoon almond extract

DIRECTIONS

[1] Preheat the oven to 425 degrees.

[2] Dump cherries into a parchment-lined loaf pan and spread evenly.

[3] Mix butter, oatmeal, flour, brown sugar, and salt in a small mixing bowl until combined. Add almonds and toss gently so that they don't get all broken up.

[4] Sprinkle the crumble over the top of the cherries. Bake for 12 to 15 minutes or until the crumble is golden brown.

[5] Whip the heavy cream, powdered sugar, and almond extract in a stand mixer fitted with a whisk attachment or using an immersion blender until soft peaks form.

[6] Serve the crumble warm, topped with a generous portion of the almond whipped cream! Store leftovers in the refrigerator.

Chantilly Vanilla Cream Puff

Growing up, my mom's go-to dessert recipe for gatherings was Dump Bars. I always thought it was the most boring dessert recipe ever—sorry, Mom! My mom never claimed to be an exceptional baker, and the bars were like a hard, dry brownie. They weren't poisonous, but they weren't craveable. But one night, our family hosted a Bible study and my mom decided to make cream puffs. They seemed so fancy, and I remember being so excited for everyone to try them. I love making them today, as they have an elevated look and taste without much effort. I was so tempted to add lemon curd, fruit, chocolate, or something different to these puffs—which you totally could. But I decided to keep them pure and unadulterated with a crispy cream puff filled with fluffy chantilly cream and dusted with powdered sugar. By the way, "chantilly cream" is just a fancy way to say extra-sweet whipped cream.

ACTIVE TIME: 30 minutes | **TOTAL TIME:** 1 hour 30 minutes | **YIELD:** 2 servings

INGREDIENTS

- ¼ cup water
- 2 tablespoons salted butter
- ¼ cup flour
- 1 large egg

Chantilly Cream:

- 1 cup heavy whipping cream
- ½ cup powdered sugar
- 1 teaspoon vanilla extract
- Powdered sugar for dusting

DIRECTIONS

[1] Preheat the oven to 425 degrees.

[2] Heat water and butter in a small saucepan until the butter is melted and the mixture is just starting to boil. Add the flour and stir vigorously until the mixture comes together in a smooth ball. Transfer it to a small mixing bowl and allow to cool for 5 minutes.

[3] Add the egg and stir until smooth. At first it may seem like the batter is lumpy and will not come together, but keep stirring until it is very smooth.

[4] Scoop the batter into two mounds using a couple of tablespoons, about 3 to 4 inches apart, on a parchment-lined baking sheet. Bake for 10 minutes and then reduce the heat to 375 degrees and bake for another 30 minutes. Open the oven door and turn the heat off. Allow to sit in the oven for 10 minutes. Cool completely.

[5] When ready to serve, make chantilly cream. In a stand mixer fitted with a whisk attachment, whip heavy cream, powdered sugar, and vanilla on medium speed until stiff peaks form. Transfer to a piping bag fitted with a large star top.

[6] Cut cream puffs in half. Use your fingers to pull out the soft inner membrane. Pipe whipped cream swirls into the bottom of each cream puff. Replace the top of the cream puff on each swirl of whipped cream.

[7] Sift powdered sugar over the top. Serve immediately. Best eaten the day of. Store leftovers in the refrigerator.

Cinnamon Dulce Ice Cream Pint

There's nothing like grabbing a pint of ice cream straight from the freezer and digging in. If you've never tried cinnamon ice cream before, you must try this recipe as soon as possible! It's a tantalizing pairing of cold ice cream and warming cinnamon. The dulce de leche swirl plays well with the strong cinnamon flavor. Grab two spoons and you are set to go. Recipe testers said that this ice cream tastes complex and the flavor seems like it would require more than four simple ingredients. To get the dulce de leche swirl in the ice cream, the recipe uses a piping bag to evenly distribute the dulce de leche over the top in ribbons before swirling it into the ice cream. If you try to add it by the spoonful, it will not swirl in but stay in big clumps.

ACTIVE TIME: 10 minutes | **TOTAL TIME:** 8 hours 10 minutes | **YIELD:** 2 servings

INGREDIENTS

- ¾ cup heavy whipping cream
- 1 teaspoon ground cinnamon
- ⅓ cup sweetened condensed milk
- ¼ cup dulce de leche

DIRECTIONS

[1] In a stand mixer fitted with a whisk attachment, beat the heavy cream and cinnamon on medium speed until stiff peaks form. Add the sweetened condensed milk and mix until it is incorporated.

[2] Transfer the dulce de leche to a piping bag. Snip a medium-size hole, and pipe squiggles over the top of the ice cream base. Gently mix the dulce de leche in, using a spatula to swirl it into the ice cream. Mix for just a few strokes to distribute it but not to deflate the cream.

[3] Transfer mixture to a pint container or any freezer-friendly container. Freeze overnight or until solid for 8 hours or overnight. This keeps well in the freezer for up to 5 days.

Summery Panna Cotta

You might be thinking, "Panna whatta?" If you've never had panna cotta, it is a simple, creamy dessert with a rich, velvety texture. Panna cotta is a no-bake dessert that relies on unflavored gelatin for a beautiful texture. Reading this recipe, it might seem like a milk-flavored Jell-O, but it has just enough gelatin to hold together, leaving you with a silky dessert with just a bit of that classic wobble. The fruity, minty, lime topping keeps this dessert interesting.

ACTIVE TIME: 15 minutes | **TOTAL TIME:** 4 hours 15 minutes | **YIELD:** 2 servings

INGREDIENTS

- 2 teaspoons water
- ¾ teaspoon unflavored gelatin
- ¾ cup heavy whipping cream
- 2 tablespoons sugar
- 1 teaspoon vanilla extract

Topping:

- 2 teaspoons freshly squeezed lime juice
- ½ teaspoon lime zest
- 2 teaspoons honey
- 1 teaspoon finely chopped fresh mint
- 1 cup fresh fruit (I prefer blackberries, diced kiwi, and blueberries)

DIRECTIONS

[1] Add water to a small bowl. Sprinkle gelatin over the surface of the water. Stir. Allow gelatin to bloom for 5 minutes.

[2] Whisk heavy cream and sugar in a microwave-safe dish. Heat for 1 minute or until just boiling. Add the bloomed gelatin and vanilla. Whisk until combined.

[3] Pour the mixture into two small parfait glasses, dividing it evenly. Refrigerate for 4 to 6 hours or until set.

[4] In a small bowl, whisk lime juice, zest, honey, and mint. Add fruit and toss to coat. Spoon the fruit over the panna cotta. Refrigerate leftovers in an airtight container.

Strawberry Cheesecake Napoleon

Crunch is the name of the game in this recipe! Puff pastry is cut into squares, pricked, layered between baking sheets, and topped with a cast-iron pan (or any heavy pan). Instead of letting puff pastry do its thing and puff up— the weight on top of it keeps it thin and makes all of the layers super crispy. The layers then alternate with a fluffy, no-bake cheesecake filling and fresh strawberries!

ACTIVE TIME: 30 minutes | **TOTAL TIME:** 1 hour 15 minutes | **YIELD:** 2 servings

INGREDIENTS

- 1 sheet puff pastry (½ of a 17.3 oz. pkg.), thawed
- 4 oz. cream cheese, softened
- ½ cup powdered sugar
- 1 teaspoon vanilla extract
- ½ cup heavy whipping cream
- 1 tablespoon strawberry jelly
- 6 medium strawberries, thinly sliced
- Powdered sugar for sifting

DIRECTIONS

[1] Preheat the oven to 400 degrees.

[2] *First, make the pastry layers.* Unfold the puff pastry sheet and use a bench scraper to cut six 3 × 3½-inch rectangles. The measurements don't need to be exact, but make sure all of the rectangles are roughly the same size. The simplest way to do this is to stack the pastry rectangles on top of each other and trim off any edges sticking out. Space them a few inches apart on a parchment-lined baking sheet and use a fork to prick holes in each piece of dough. (You will have a bit of dough left over. You could top it with some jam and bake for a yummy breakfast pastry!)

[3] Place another piece of parchment on top of the pricked dough and another baking sheet on top. Place a heavy pan like a cast-iron skillet on top to weigh the sheet pan down. This helps prevent the pastry from puffing up and keeps it nice and crunchy. Bake for 20 to 25 minutes or until golden brown. Cool completely.

[4] *Next, make the filling.* Beat cream cheese, powdered sugar, and vanilla in a stand mixer fitted with the paddle attachment on low speed until smooth and no lumps remain.

[5] Remove the paddle attachment and swap in the whisk attachment on the stand mixer. Add heavy cream and whip until thick. Transfer to a piping bag fitted with a large round tip.

[6] Heat the jelly in a small microwave-safe bowl for 15 seconds. Add the strawberry slices and toss to coat.

[7] *Finally, put it all together.* To assemble the desserts, place one rectangle of crispy pastry on each serving plate. Pipe dollops of cheesecake filling onto each rectangle.

[8] Arrange strawberry slices on top. Pipe a squiggle of cheesecake filling on top of the strawberries to keep the second layer from sliding.

[9] Place the second rectangle of pastry onto each dessert. Again, pipe the filling and arrange strawberry slices on top.

[10] Place the third pastry layer on each dessert. Pipe a few dollops of filling in the center of each pastry. Arrange a few strawberry slices on top.

[11] Sift powdered sugar over the top.

[12] Serve immediately. Best eaten the day of. Store leftovers in the refrigerator.

Apple Galette

One priority for me when baking is not having to buy lots of special pans and dishes and only using them for one specific recipe. This can be a challenge when creating recipes for just two people, making this free-form apple galette the perfect "no special equipment needed" dessert! A simple four-ingredient pie crust is rolled into a rough circle and layered with spiced apple slices. The crust comes together by pulling up the excess dough around the apples, creating a beautiful rustic apple pie for two. For me, pie crust can be more of a "take it or leave it" type of thing—nothing special. Not this crust. It's flaky and crispy, and the raw sugar crunch takes it to another level! If you don't have raw sugar, use regular granulated sugar.

ACTIVE TIME: 25 minutes | **TOTAL TIME:** 1 hour 10 minutes | **YIELD:** 2 servings

INGREDIENTS

- ¾ cup all-purpose flour, plus extra for sprinkling
- ⅓ cup cold salted butter
- 1 large egg, beaten, divided
- 3 tablespoons whole milk
- 1 large Granny Smith apple, peeled and thinly sliced
- 1 tablespoon sugar
- 1 teaspoon cinnamon
- 1 tablespoon salted butter
- 2 teaspoons raw sugar
- Vanilla ice cream

DIRECTIONS

[1] Add the flour to a medium-size mixing bowl. Grate the butter into the flour. Use your fingers to break up the butter into small pieces throughout the flour. This should just take a minute or so. Be careful to move quickly so you don't melt the butter with the warmth of your hands.

[2] Add 1 tablespoon of the beaten egg. Set aside the remaining beaten egg. Add the milk and stir using a spatula until combined.

[3] Place a piece of plastic wrap on your work surface. Transfer the dough into the center of the wrap. Bring the sides of the plastic wrap up and over the dough. Press into a disk. Refrigerate for 20 minutes.

[4] Preheat the oven to 375 degrees.

[5] Lightly flour a piece of parchment paper. Unwrap dough and place in the center of the floured parchment. Flour a rolling pin, and roll the dough until it is about ⅛-inch thick or about 9 inches in diameter.

[6] Toss the apple slices, sugar, and cinnamon.

[7] Arrange the apple slices on the pie dough. I like to stack 5 to 6 slices together, fan them out, and place them on the crust. Leave a two-inch border of pie dough around the edges.

[8] Fold the dough up over the filling, tucking as you fold. Slice butter into thin slices and place over the apples.

[9] Take the remaining beaten egg and brush it over the folded edges of the galette dough. Sprinkle it with raw sugar. Place the parchment onto a baking sheet and bake for 20 to 25 minutes or until golden brown.

[10] Allow the galette to cool slightly.

[11] Top with vanilla ice cream and serve warm. Store leftovers in the refrigerator.

Almond Wedding Cake

Make this to celebrate an anniversary. At first glance, this might look like a typical white wedding cake, but it is anything but. The cake is a flavorful almond cake that is moist and layered with a classic vanilla almond buttercream. You can relive your wedding memories and feed each other, but whatever you do, don't smash this in their face! It's way too yummy to waste. I found it hard to frost these tiny cake squares with my big offset spatula, so I opted for a piping bag instead. If you don't have a piping bag, use a butter knife to spread the frosting between the layers instead.

ACTIVE TIME: 30 minutes | **TOTAL TIME:** 1 hour 25 minutes | **YIELD:** 2 servings

INGREDIENTS

Cake:

- 2 oz. almond paste
- 6 tablespoons salted butter, softened
- ⅓ cup sugar
- 2 large eggs
- ¼ teaspoon vanilla extract
- ¼ cup all-purpose flour
- ¼ teaspoon baking powder

Frosting:

- 1 cup powdered sugar
- ¼ cup salted butter, softened
- 1 teaspoon heavy whipping cream
- ½ teaspoon vanilla extract
- ¼ teaspoon almond extract

DIRECTIONS

[1] Preheat the oven to 325 degrees.

[2] *Make the cake.* In a stand mixer fitted with the paddle attachment, cream the almond paste, butter, and sugar until smooth and fluffy.

[3] Add the eggs and vanilla. Mix on medium speed until incorporated. Increase the speed to medium-high and beat for 1 to 2 minutes or until thick, fluffy, and light in color.

[4] Add the flour and baking powder and mix on low until just combined. Spread the batter into a greased and parchment-lined 9 × 4-inch loaf pan. Bake for 20 to 25 minutes until golden and set. If the cake is still wobbly in the center, continue baking. Cool completely. Run a butter knife around the edges to separate any cake stuck to the pan. Place in the freezer for 20 minutes.

[5] *Make the frosting.* While the cake is chilling, beat the powdered sugar and butter in a stand mixer fitted with the paddle attachment until smooth. Add the heavy cream, vanilla, and almond extract and mix until combined. Increase the speed to medium-high for 1 minute. Transfer frosting to a piping bag fitted with a large round tip.

[6] Remove the cake from the freezer and invert it onto your work surface. Trim about ¼ inch off each side. Then, cut the rectangle as best you can into three equal pieces. Stack the cake pieces on top of each other and trim any bits that are sticking out so that you have three equal pieces.

[7] Place a piece of plastic wrap on your work surface. Place one piece of cake down. Pipe lines of frosting over the cake. Place the next cake layer and gently press down. Repeat until you finish stacking all your cake layers. Finish with more frosting on top. Pull the plastic up around the cake and wrap the cake. Refrigerate for 30 minutes. Unwrap the cake. Use a sharp knife dipped in hot water to cut the cake into two slices. Place the cut side up on your desired plates. Allow to sit at room temperature for 10 minutes. Serve. Store leftovers in an airtight container.

Decadent Chocolate Cake

Picture this: one giant piece of chocolate cake, two forks, and you and your significant other meeting in the middle with Lady and the Tramp *vibes. Can it get any more perfect? I don't think so. This cake is chocolate on chocolate on chocolate. It starts with layers of dense chocolate cake, rich chocolate ganache, layered with fluffy chocolate whipped cream, and topped with bittersweet chocolate curls.*

ACTIVE TIME: 25 minutes | **TOTAL TIME:** 55 minutes | **YIELD:** 2 servings

INGREDIENTS

Chocolate Cake:

- ¾ cup all-purpose flour
- ½ cup sugar
- 2 tablespoons unsweetened cocoa powder
- Pinch of salt
- ½ teaspoon baking soda
- 1 teaspoon vanilla extract
- ½ cup cold water
- ½ teaspoon distilled white vinegar
- 2½ tablespoons canola oil
- ½ teaspoon instant coffee

Ganache:

- ½ cup semisweet chocolate chips
- ¼ cup heavy whipping cream

Chocolate Whipped Cream:

- 1¼ cups heavy whipping cream
- 1 cup powdered sugar
- 3 tablespoons unsweetened cocoa powder

Chocolate Curls:

- ½ ounce bittersweet chocolate (optional)

DIRECTIONS

[1] Preheat the oven to 350 degrees.

[2] *First, bake the cake.* Whisk flour, sugar, cocoa, salt, and baking soda in a medium-size mixing bowl until combined.

[3] Add vanilla, water, vinegar, oil, and instant coffee and whisk until smooth. Pour into a greased and parchment-lined 9-inch square pan and bake for 10 to 12 minutes or until the cake springs back when gently pressed. Allow to cool.

[4] *While the cake bakes, make the ganache.* Dump chocolate chips into a small heatproof dish. Heat the heavy cream in the microwave for 20 seconds and pour over the chocolate. Let sit for 1 minute and stir until smooth. If lumps remain, microwave for another 30 seconds and stir. Allow to cool.

[5] *Then, make the chocolate whipped cream frosting and assemble the cake.* In a stand mixer fitted with a whisk attachment, whip the heavy cream, powdered sugar, and cocoa until stiff peaks form. Transfer to a piping bag fitted with a round tip.

[6] Remove the cake from the pan and cut it into four even squares using a bread knife. Set one square aside. I prefer to use only three layers, as it can get tippy if you go too high.

[7] Place one square on the serving plate. Using an offset spatula, spread about a third of the ganache in an even layer. Pipe dollops of the chocolate whipped cream. Place another square of chocolate cake on top and repeat two more times.

[8] *If desired, finish with chocolate curls.* Scrape a vegetable peeler on the bittersweet chocolate over the cake to create chocolate curls. Store in the refrigerator until ready to serve. Store leftovers in the fridge.

Chocolate Shell Crème

Crème brûlée is known as a fancy, romantic dessert, so it's a perfect fit for this chapter. But this book is all about a more minimal kitchen setup, and I know many people don't have a kitchen torch (or any kind of torch for that matter) to get that crunchy sugar topping. So I decided to eliminate the brûlée topping, but without it, this dessert lacked the signature crunch—enter the chocolate shell. Not only does the chocolate shell lend a nice snap to this otherwise creamy dessert, but it also adds a delicious chocolate flavor.

ACTIVE TIME: 15 minutes | **TOTAL TIME:** 2 hours | **YIELD:** 2 servings

INGREDIENTS

- 1 cup heavy whipping cream
- 3 egg yolks
- ¼ cup sugar
- 1 teaspoon vanilla extract
- Pinch of salt
- Boiling water

Chocolate Shell:

- 2 tablespoons mini semisweet chocolate chips
- 1 teaspoon coconut oil

DIRECTIONS

[1] Preheat the oven to 325 degrees.

[2] Add the heavy cream to a microwave-safe container and microwave for about 1 minute or until hot and steamy but not boiling.

[3] While the cream is heating, whisk egg yolks and sugar in a small bowl until smooth.

[4] Slowly drizzle the hot cream into the yolks, whisking constantly until all the cream has been added.

[5] Stir in the vanilla and salt.

[6] Place two 8-ounce ramekins into a loaf pan. Fill the ramekins with the custard mixture. Pour boiling water into the loaf pan a little over an inch deep, being careful not to get any into the ramekins. Carefully transfer to the oven and bake for 40 to 45 minutes, or until the edge of the custard is set but the center is wobbly.

[7] Remove from the water bath and allow to cool slightly, then place custards in the fridge until completely chilled.

[8] In a microwave-safe dish, heat chocolate and coconut oil for 30 seconds. Stir until smooth. Pour half of the melted chocolate shell on one of the custards, and swirl until the custard is covered with a thin layer of chocolate. Repeat with the second custard. Refrigerate until the shell is set. Serve chilled. Store leftovers in the refrigerator.

Blender Chocolate Mousse

This chocolate mousse comes together in a snap and packs a serious chocolatey punch! Classic chocolate mousse requires you to separate your eggs, whip the egg whites, whip the cream, temper the egg yolks, and gently fold it all together. This variation eliminates all those steps and accomplishes a similar outcome in seconds. The boiling water tempers the egg and melts the chocolate, and the blender aerates the mixture. After it's chilled, you can eat it straight up or top it with some whipped cream, raspberries, and chocolate curls to break up the intense chocolate flavor.

ACTIVE TIME: 10 minutes | **TOTAL TIME:** 2 hours 10 minutes | **YIELD:** 2 servings

INGREDIENTS

- 1 large egg
- 4 ounces semisweet chocolate, very finely chopped
- ½ teaspoon instant coffee
- ¼ cup boiling water
- ½ cup heavy whipping cream
- 1 teaspoon vanilla extract
- Pinch of salt
- Whipped cream, fresh raspberries, and chocolate curls (optional)

DIRECTIONS

[1] Blend the egg, chocolate, and instant coffee until smooth or until very few lumps remain, depending on the power of your blender. Slowly stream the water into the chocolate and blend until completely smooth.

[2] Add the heavy cream, vanilla, and salt and blend until combined. Split the mousse into two ramekins or parfait glasses that hold at least 6 ounces and refrigerate for at least 2 hours. Top with whipped cream, raspberries, and chocolate curls, if desired. Serve. Store leftovers in the refrigerator.

Simple Ways to Make Your Partner Feel Special

As I said at the beginning of the chapter, I'm not exactly an expert on love, so I brought in some of the gals from my family to share a few simple ways to make your spouse feel loved. These are not elaborate date nights but little ways to say, "I appreciate you and am thinking of you!"

> *Send him a sweet text of encouragement when he has lots happening in his day. Or send him off with a treat and coffee when he leaves.*
> **—AUNT LINDA**

Linda's husband Erling has big days of work as an order buyer at the sale barn, and a text is perfect for a quick dose of encouragement in the midst of a hectic day. And you definitely can't go wrong with coffee and a treat! Check out chapter 7 for some tasty portable treat recipes.

> *I like to leave handwritten notes of encouragement or just "love you" reminders. I always try to make him smile. In our house, whoever makes the first pot of coffee in the morning is saying, "I love you!" If the boys have been up in the night, Cody will get up and make me coffee before I get up to help me get going. It means so much. And if Cody is the tired one, I will make a pot of coffee, pour his cup of joe, and add his big dash of creamer.*
> **—MY SISTER TRICIA**

I love the idea of simple handwritten notes, and a little humor never hurt anything. Also, I'm pretty sure there are six love languages—coffee being the sixth.

> *In busy seasons of family life, when the calendar is chock full of practices, games, chores, and homework, there's little room left for extravagant plans. It might not be a time of life marked by expensive gifts and fancy date nights, but it can be known for loving sacrificially. Gifts of quality*

time and special attention can be even more meaningful when it means giving precious free time and effort to prioritize your loved one! Making someone feel lavishly loved could be as simple as a meal at home with decorations and cards of compliments from the little ones or a distraction-free night where work and "extras" are cleared to make room for rest and favorite foods.

—MY COUSIN MONICA

I think a lot of wives could relate to Monica's full schedule. She and her husband, Andy, have six kids and are busy with school and sports. On top of that, Andy is a pastor, and as a team, they do a great job of welcoming people into their homes and being involved in so many people's lives. I love how she shared that making things feel special is not going out on a big date night but clearing the calendar and staying home together!

To let Gary know I'm thinking about him even if we're in a group of people, I rest my hand on him and gently press each fingertip down one at a time, communicating: I Love You Very Much!

—MY MOM, LORI

Sweet and simple—I'm sold!

If one of us goes to town without the other, we will pick up a Mounds candy bar and bring it home. We split the package and enjoy it together with coffee or sparkling water.

—MY MOM, LORI

This is especially relevant when you live out in the country but works even if you're in town. If you see a little treat you know your spouse would be into—pick it up for them! Not only do they get treated, but they know you were thinking of them.

Bread
Oat meal Cookies
1 C shortening
1C raisins

CHAPTER 4

Village People

[NOSTALGIC DESSERTS]

You've heard the saying, "It takes a village." I can totally see this being true in my own life. It takes parents, grandparents, aunts, uncles, extended family, friends, teachers, pastors, coaches, and the list goes on to bring a child from birth to adulthood and beyond. These people have taught, encouraged, chastised, and developed me into the person I am today. This is true for each of us, and while each of our "villages" may look different, we all have people in our lives who shape us.

I am so thankful for each of these people, and I want them to know how special they are. It's nice to celebrate on established holidays, but you don't need to wait for a specific date to celebrate these VIPs. You can honor them by giving them a call and letting them know how they impacted you or by dropping a note in the mail thanking them for a specific difference they made in your life. Or you can make one of the recipes from this chapter and drop by their house for a visit.

Now these "village people" are not old, but they are "older." So, this chapter is all about nostalgic recipes. Recipes that have stood the test of time, many of them coming from Grandma Wilken's and Grandma Pearl's recipe collections. I love how food has the power to take us back to a moment, and these recipes take me back to my grandma's kitchen.

Shortcut Raspberry Kuchen

I absolutely love South Dakota! Other than college, I have lived here all my life and, Lord willing, I will never leave—well, not permanently at least. (I'm not against a trip to the beach!) And do you know what the South Dakota state dessert is? Kuchen! If you've never had kuchen, it has a yeast crust with a slight chew, topped with fruit (although my favorite type of kuchen is cottage cheese—yes, this is a thing!), a not-too-sweet custard, and cinnamon sugar. Kuchen is a big deal here in South Dakota; there are entire grocery freezer cases dedicated to it. These people REALLY love their kuchen. I was looking for a good kuchen recipe when I had a follower recommend a Facebook group called "Germans from Russia Food and Culture." I realized that not only is this our state dessert, it is also the dessert of my people (well at least Grandma Pearl's side of the family, because they are just that—Germans from Russia!). Anyway, there were no less than 30 different kuchen recipes on this page, and this is what I came up with. I was focused on making doable dessert recipes in this book, so I tried swapping in frozen bread dough in place of the homemade dough, and it is shocking how similar the result is.

ACTIVE TIME: 10 minutes | **TOTAL TIME:** 2 hours | **YIELD:** 2 kuchens, 12–16 servings

INGREDIENTS

- 1 (1 lb.) loaf frozen bread dough (thawed in the refrigerator 8 hours or overnight)
- 2 eggs
- ½ cup granulated sugar
- ½ cup heavy whipping cream
- ½ cup sour cream
- 1 tablespoon all-purpose flour
- 1⅓ cups raspberries, fresh or frozen

Cinnamon Sugar:

- 1 teaspoon sugar
- ¼ teaspoon ground cinnamon

DIRECTIONS

[1] Preheat the oven to 350 degrees.

[2] Prepare two 9-inch pie pans by spraying them lightly with nonstick cooking spray. Divide the dough into two equal portions, and on a floured surface, roll each portion into a circle about ¼ to ⅛ inches thick or about 10 inches in diameter. Do not knead or work the dough, as it will quickly lose its elasticity. If your dough keeps shrinking, allow it to rest for 10 minutes on your counter and then roll it again. Place the dough into the prepared pie pans, pressing the dough about an inch up the sides.

[3] Whisk the eggs, sugar, heavy cream, sour cream, and flour until smooth.

[4] If your dough has shrunk at all, press it back up the sides of the pan. Sprinkle ⅔ cup raspberries on each crust.

[5] Pour the filling over the raspberries, dividing it evenly between the two pans.

[6] In a small dish, mix the cinnamon sugar and sprinkle it over the top of each kuchen, dividing it evenly between the two pans.

[7] Bake for 20 to 25 minutes, or until the crust is golden and the kuchen is mostly set but has a slight jiggle in the center. Allow it to cool at room temperature until you can handle it, and then transfer it to the refrigerator until chilled. Cut into wedges and serve cold. Store leftovers in the fridge.

Daddy's Favorite Gingersnaps

My sisters entered these gingersnap cookies into the county fair numerous times. This is Grandma Wilken's recipe, and she made these cookies countless times for my dad growing up. I think these cookies are surprising to people, as it would seem that the best cookies must have chocolate. But these cookies prove that the combination of molasses and ginger is a winner, and the sugar coating adds a nice crispness. The result is a cookie that is crisp on the edges and chewy in the center.

ACTIVE TIME: 10 minutes | **TOTAL TIME:** 55 minutes | **YIELD:** 2 dozen cookies

INGREDIENTS

- ¾ cup salted butter, softened
- 1 cup sugar
- 1 large egg
- ¼ cup molasses
- 2 cups all-purpose flour
- 2 teaspoons baking soda
- 1 teaspoon cinnamon
- 1 teaspoon ground ginger
- ½ teaspoon salt
- Extra sugar for coating

DIRECTIONS

[1] Preheat the oven to 350 degrees.

[2] In a medium-size bowl, cream butter and sugar until smooth and thick.

[3] Add the egg and molasses and stir until smooth.

[4] Dump in flour, baking soda, cinnamon, ginger, and salt. Mix until combined.

[5] Refrigerate the dough for 30 minutes.

[6] Use a 1½-tablespoon scoop to portion the dough into balls, rolling each portion in sugar. Space cookie dough about 1 to 2 inches apart on a parchment-lined baking sheet and bake for 9 to 12 minutes or until browned on the edges and slightly underbaked in the center. Bake in batches until all of the dough has been baked. Store leftovers in an airtight container.

Strawberry Shortcake

Grandma Wilken's go-to dessert when I was growing up was boxed yellow cake, frozen strawberries sliced up, and topped with a big tub of Cool Whip. This recipe is an ode to that winning combination. Instead of a yellow cake mix, this from-scratch cake starts with the reverse creaming method. Simply put: Mix all the dry ingredients, then add the butter and mix until the mixture looks like wet sand. Add the wet ingredients and mix until just combined. The final product is a tender, buttery cake. The edges are caramelized and a bit crispy. This cake is extraordinary and could be enjoyed on its own, but I finish it with real whipped cream and fresh strawberries in place of the original Cool Whip and frozen strawberries. Although if you're making this out of season, I would opt for frozen strawberries, sliced and thawed.

ACTIVE TIME: 30 minutes | **TOTAL TIME:** 1 hour 40 minutes | **YIELD:** 9 servings

INGREDIENTS

- 1⅓ cups sugar
- 1 cup + 1 tablespoon all-purpose flour
- 3 tablespoons cornstarch
- 1¼ teaspoons baking powder
- ⅛ teaspoon baking soda
- ¼ teaspoon salt
- ½ cup salted butter, softened and cut into about 6 chunks
- 1 large egg
- 1 large egg yolk
- ½ cup sour cream
- ½ cup whole milk
- 1 teaspoon vanilla extract
- 1 lb. fresh strawberries
- 1 tablespoon sugar

Whipped Cream:

- 1½ cups heavy whipping cream
- ⅓ cup powdered sugar
- 1 teaspoon vanilla extract

DIRECTIONS

[1] Preheat the oven to 350 degrees.

[2] Mix sugar, flour, cornstarch, baking powder, baking soda, and salt in a stand mixer fitted with a paddle attachment on low speed until combined. Add the chunks of butter and stir until the mixture looks like wet sand.

[3] In a separate bowl whisk the egg, egg yolk, sour cream, milk, and vanilla until smooth.

[4] Add the liquid mixture to the dry mixture and stir until just combined. Be careful not to overmix. You will see lumps of butter and that's totally normal!

[5] Pour the batter into a parchment-lined and greased 9-inch square pan and bake for 35 to 40 minutes or until a toothpick inserted comes out with a few moist crumbs. Allow to cool.

[6] Hull and slice the strawberries. Sprinkle the sugar over the berries. Stir and allow them to sit for 5 minutes.

[7] Whip the heavy cream, powdered sugar, and vanilla in a stand mixer fitted with a whisk attachment until soft peaks form.

[8] When ready to serve, cut the cake into nine squares. Cut each square in half horizontally and open each cake square flat on the dessert plates (kind of like a hamburger bun).

[9] Top cake with generous portions of whipped cream and sliced strawberries. Serve immediately. Store the cake in an airtight container and the whipped cream and strawberries in the refrigerator.

NOTE: My grandad was a big fan of this combo but preferred angel food cake over yellow cake. His mom had made it for his birthday when he was growing up and, considering he was born in the 1920s and everything in his life had changed since then—electricity, automobiles, refrigeration, and so on—it was pretty remarkable that he could still eat the exact same thing for his birthday at 95 as he did at age 5. I really wanted to include angel food cake in this book, but truthfully I've always made it from a box mix. When I tested an angel food cake recipe, I quickly realized that I prefer the boxed cake version of angel food cake (I know, probably an unpopular opinion) over the "from-scratch recipe." As special as this story is to me, I wouldn't share the recipe if I wasn't excited about it. So, basically, if you want to eat your strawberry shortcake "grandad style," swap in angel food cake in place of yellow cake.

Chocolate Crazy Cake with Penuche Frosting

I started a series on my Instagram of trying recipes from Grandma Wilken's recipe box. One video I created in the series was of me trying this penuche frosting that my grandma had received from her sister-in-law, Janet Wilken. This video went viral, but only partially for the taste. Don't get me wrong, this recipe is incredible. The rich chocolate, the sweet penuche frosting, and the flaky sea salt balances it all out. It's truly incredible! But the other reason it took off was because of how I pronounced penuche. I grew up with my family pronouncing it pen-oosh, but everyone in the comments said it should be pen-oo-che. Regardless of how you pronounce penuche, this frosting is one to add to your repertoire.

ACTIVE TIME: 20 minutes | **TOTAL TIME:** 1 hour 20 minutes | **YIELD:** 8–12 wedges

INGREDIENTS

- Chocolate Crazy Cake (page 214)

Frosting:

- ¼ cup salted butter
- ½ cup dark brown sugar
- 3 tablespoons heavy whipping cream, divided
- ¾ cup powdered sugar, sifted
- Flaky sea salt (optional)

DIRECTIONS

[1] Preheat the oven to 350 degrees.

[2] Prepare the Chocolate Crazy Cake batter according to the recipe. Pour the batter into a greased and parchment-lined 8-inch round cake pan. Bake for 25 to 30 minutes. Cool completely.

[3] In a medium saucepan over low heat, melt the butter. You do not want to let the butter get too hot. Add the brown sugar and whisk until combined. Continue to heat over medium low heat, stirring occasionally.

[4] Once the caramel starts bubbling, cook for 2 minutes, stirring constantly.

[5] Stir in 2 tablespoons of heavy cream. Bring to a boil and remove from the heat. Cool to room temperature.

[6] Add the powdered sugar to the caramel and whisk until smooth. Add the remaining tablespoon of heavy cream and whisk vigorously until completely combined and thick.

[7] Run a butter knife around the edge of the cooled cake and invert the pan on your desired plate or cake stand. Remove the pan and peel off the parchment. Spread the frosting over the chocolate cake using an offset spatula and sprinkle with flaky sea salt, if desired. Cut into wedges and serve. Store leftovers in an airtight container.

Chocolate Revel Bars

This classic bar is a family favorite and always makes an appearance at our family's bull sale—compliments of my aunt Linda. It's a simple oat crust, with a rich chocolate filling, and more of the same oat crust crumbled on top. Not to mention—these bars travel well, freeze excellently, and use simple ingredients. I like to eat them cold from the fridge, as this makes them denser, chewier, and fudgier.

ACTIVE TIME: 15 minutes | **TOTAL TIME:** 40 minutes plus cooling | **YIELD:** 16 squares (2 × 2 inches)

INGREDIENTS

Crust:

- 1 cup dark brown sugar
- ½ cup salted butter, softened
- 1 large egg
- 1 teaspoon vanilla extract
- 1½ cups quick-cooking oats
- 1¼ cups all-purpose flour
- ½ teaspoon baking soda
- Pinch of salt

Filling:

- 1 cup sweetened condensed milk
- ¾ cup semisweet chocolate chips
- 1 tablespoon salted butter
- Pinch of salt
- 1 teaspoon vanilla extract

DIRECTIONS

[1] Preheat the oven to 350 degrees.

[2] Add the crust ingredients to a stand mixer fitted with the paddle attachment and mix on low speed until combined. Set aside.

[3] Heat sweetened condensed milk, chocolate chips, and remaining butter in a microwave-safe bowl for 30 seconds and stir. Microwave for another 30 seconds and stir. Repeat until the chocolate is melted. Add salt and vanilla. Stir until combined.

[4] Dump two-thirds of the crust into a parchment-lined 8-inch square pan and use your hands to press the mixture evenly into the bottom of the pan.

[5] Pour the filling over the crust and spread evenly.

[6] Sprinkle the remaining crust mixture over the top using your fingers.

[7] Bake for 20 to 25 minutes until the oats are golden and if you give the pan a jiggle, the chocolate is set on the edges with just a slight wobble in the center. Cool completely. Cut into squares and serve. Store leftovers in an airtight container.

Funeral Bars

In small communities like ours, the "church ladies" are often asked to make a pan or two of bars for the lunch after a funeral. When asked to supply a pan of bars, my aunt Linda typically makes her Mixed Nut Bars. Apparently, it became such a common occurrence, we started calling them Funeral Bars. So just to clarify—there's nothing morbid about this treat and it would be great to serve for all sorts of occasions—not just funerals! I did tweak the recipe to create a lovely honey and brown sugar syrup to bind the salty mixed nuts with a buttery shortbread crust. If you're a fan of the salty/sweet combo—this recipe will be your new favorite!

ACTIVE TIME: 10 minutes | **TOTAL TIME:** 1 hour 15 minutes | **YIELD:** 16 bars (2 × 2-inch squares)

INGREDIENTS

Crust:

- ½ cup salted butter, melted
- ¼ cup sugar
- Pinch of salt
- 1 cup all-purpose flour

Filling:

- ¼ cup salted butter, melted
- ⅓ cup dark brown sugar
- ⅓ cup honey
- 1 tablespoon heavy whipping cream
- ½ teaspoon vanilla extract
- 1 cup mixed nuts

DIRECTIONS

[1] Preheat the oven to 325 degrees.

[2] *Prepare the crust.* Mix the butter, sugar, and salt in a medium-size mixing bowl until combined. Add the flour and stir until smooth.

[3] Dump into a parchment-lined 8-inch square pan and press into the bottom of the pan using your fingers or a spatula. Bake for 15 to 17 minutes or until lightly browned.

[4] *Prepare the filling.* While the crust is baking, make the filling. In a medium-size microwave-safe bowl add the butter, brown sugar, honey, and heavy cream. Heat in the microwave for 30 seconds and whisk until smooth. Repeat until the filling is boiling when you pull it out of the microwave.

[5] Stir in the vanilla and mixed nuts. Pour over the crust.

[6] Increase oven temperature to 350 degrees. Bake for another 18 to 20 minutes or until bubbling vigorously and mostly set. Cool completely. Cut into squares. Store leftovers in an airtight container.

Pumpkin Roll

This pumpkin roll cake might seem kind of intimidating, but once you know a few tips and tricks, it's totally doable. So here are five rapid-fire tips for roll cakes. First, make sure that your pan is greased and lined with parchment. Second, take the time to set up your "rolling station" before your cake comes out of the oven. It has to be rolled while it is still very hot. Third, let your cake cool completely rolled up in a towel. Don't unroll it too soon. Fourth, when it's time to unroll it, unroll it very slowly—and I repeat...very slowly—unroll your cooled cake. Fifth, don't let cracks get you down. Your cake shouldn't crack, but if it does, roll it up the best you can and the frosting will help hold it together. And a quick bonus tip...for best results make it the day before. This helps the frosting and the cake become one.

ACTIVE TIME: 30 minutes | **TOTAL TIME:** 3 hours 50 minutes | **YIELD:** 12 pieces

INGREDIENTS

Cake:

- 5 large eggs
- 1⅔ cups granulated sugar
- 1 cup canned pumpkin puree
- 1¼ cups all-purpose flour
- 1 teaspoon baking powder
- ¾ teaspoon baking soda
- 2 teaspoons ground cinnamon
- ¾ teaspoon ground cloves
- ¼ teaspoon salt
- Powdered sugar for sprinkling

Frosting:

- ½ cup salted butter, softened
- 1 (8 oz.) package cream cheese, softened
- 2 cups powdered sugar
- 2 teaspoons vanilla extract

DIRECTIONS

[1] Preheat the oven to 350 degrees.

[2] In a large mixing bowl, whisk eggs, sugar, and pumpkin until smooth.

[3] Add the flour, baking powder, baking soda, cinnamon, cloves, and salt and stir until completely combined.

[4] Pour the batter into a greased and parchment-lined rimmed 13 × 18-inch baking sheet. Use an offset spatula to spread the batter into an even layer. Bake for 15 to 20 minutes or until the cake springs back when gently pressed.

[5] While the cake is baking, prepare the rolling station. Place a tea towel on your counter and use a sieve to sprinkle powdered sugar over it. This helps keep the cake from sticking to the towel. Have a butter knife and potholders ready to go.

[6] When the cake comes out of the oven, immediately run a butter knife around the edge of the pan. Holding the pan with your potholders, invert the cake (short side facing you) onto the tea towel, being mindful to leave a couple inches of towel showing on the side nearest you. Remove the pan. Slowly peel off the parchment paper. Fold the extra towel edge nearest you over the cake and roll the cake into the towel until the entire cake is rolled. Set aside and cool completely, about 1 to 2 hours.

[7] In a stand mixer fitted with a paddle attachment, cream butter and cream cheese until smooth and no lumps remain. Add the powdered sugar and vanilla and mix until smooth.

[8] Carefully unroll the cooled cake. Scoop the frosting over the cake and use an offset spatula to smooth it out.

[9] Roll the cake back up, being careful to roll slowly, starting from the same end as before.

[10] Wrap the cake in plastic wrap and refrigerate for at least 1 hour, but I prefer to refrigerate it overnight.

[11] When you are ready to serve the cake, place the roll on your serving dish and use a serrated knife to cut it into 1-inch-thick pieces. Serve. Store leftovers in the fridge.

Elevated Dump Bars

You read that right. I just used the words "elevated" and "dump" in the same recipe title. If you missed me ragging on my mom's Dump Bars back on page 59, you can head there to get the backstory. I've taken what seemed like the lamest dessert ever and changed it into something much tastier without losing the one-bowl appeal.

ACTIVE TIME: 5 minutes | **TOTAL TIME:** 30 minutes | **YIELD:** 16 squares (2 × 2 inches)

INGREDIENTS

- ½ cup salted butter, melted
- ½ cup sugar
- ½ cup dark brown sugar
- 2 large eggs
- 2 teaspoons vanilla extract
- ½ cup all-purpose flour
- ½ cup cocoa powder
- ½ teaspoon instant coffee
- ½ cup butterscotch chips
- Flaky sea salt

DIRECTIONS

[1] Preheat the oven to 350 degrees.

[2] Mix butter, sugar, brown sugar, eggs, vanilla, flour, cocoa, and instant coffee in a medium-size mixing bowl until combined. Pour into a parchment-lined 8-inch square pan. Sprinkle butterscotch chips over the top.

[3] Bake for 20 to 25 minutes or until set.

[4] Top with flaky sea salt. Allow to cool slightly and cut into squares. Store leftovers in an airtight container.

Peanut Butter Bars

This is another recipe from Grandma Wilken's recipe box. It's simple and very rich. The graham cracker crumbs add a bit of texture to these otherwise soft bars. These bars are best served cold, as they will lose their shape if they get too warm.

ACTIVE TIME: 10 minutes | **TOTAL TIME:** 30 minutes | **YIELD:** 16 squares (2 × 2 inches)

INGREDIENTS

- 1¼ cup salted butter, divided
- 1 cup creamy peanut butter
- 2 cups graham cracker crumbs
- 2 cups powdered sugar
- ¼ cup heavy whipping cream
- ½ cup semisweet chocolate chips

DIRECTIONS

[1] Melt 1 cup of butter in a microwave-safe dish.

[2] Add the peanut butter and stir using a rubber spatula until combined. Add the graham cracker crumbs and powdered sugar and mix until combined. Dump the mixture into an ungreased 9 × 13-inch pan and spread into an even layer using an offset spatula. Refrigerate for 10 minutes.

[3] To make the topping, heat the remaining ¼ cup butter and the heavy cream in the microwave for 45 seconds or until the butter is melted and the mixture is hot and steamy. Add the chocolate chips and let mixture sit for 1 minute. Stir until no lumps remain. Pour the chocolate over the peanut butter layer and spread using an offset spatula. Refrigerate until the chocolate is set. Cut into squares and serve. Refrigerate leftovers in an airtight container.

Coconut Cream Pie

When I was 13 years old, my dad leased land by the Crow Buttes Mercantile. After we worked cows for the day, we would stop in and get a bite to eat. I would describe it like a general store you would see in the Old West (it wasn't a decor theme...I think it actually hadn't been updated since then). We would order chicken strips and they would come out in baskets with french fries looking super glossy and shiny from all the grease—not complaining! One of the times we were in there, I picked up a little cookbook on pies, and I read that book cover to cover so many times. (Still do!) This book introduced me to coconut cream pie, and while I've tweaked the recipe since then, it still holds a special place for me.

ACTIVE TIME: 45 minutes | **TOTAL TIME:** 3 hours | **YIELD:** 8–10 servings

INGREDIENTS

Crust:

- 1½ cups graham cracker crumbs
- ¼ cup sugar
- 6 tablespoons salted butter, melted

Filling:

- Coconut Cream (page 213)
- ⅓ cup unsweetened coconut flakes
- 1½ cups heavy whipping cream
- ½ cup powdered sugar
- 2 teaspoons vanilla extract

DIRECTIONS

[1] Toss the graham cracker crumbs, sugar, and butter in a medium-size mixing bowl until evenly coated. Press the crumbs into a 9-inch pie pan using a measuring cup to press the crust up the sides. Refrigerate the crust while you prepare the filling.

[2] Prepare Coconut Cream according to recipe directions. Pour it into the prepared crust and spread into an even layer. Cover with plastic wrap and press it to the surface of the filling. Refrigerate until chilled, about 2 to 4 hours.

[3] Spread coconut flakes on a sheet pan. Toast the coconut in the oven at 350 degrees for about 5 minutes or until golden. Keep a close eye so that you don't burn the coconut. Cool completely.

[4] Whip cream, powdered sugar, and vanilla in a stand mixer fitted with the whisk attachment until stiff peaks form. Spread whipped cream over the coconut custard. Sprinkle the pie with toasted coconut. Keep in the refrigerator until ready to serve. Store leftovers in the fridge.

NOTE: Make the crust, filling, and toast the coconut the day before. Then, when it's time to serve, make and spread the whipped cream and sprinkle on the toasted coconut.

Blueberry Swirl Cheesecake

Believe it or not, when I was ten years old and the internet and Pinterest weren't part of my life, getting the once-a-month Taste of Home *magazine was something I truly looked forward to. I opened the bundle of mail one day and pulled out the magazine. On the cover was a gorgeous blueberry swirl cheesecake. I took the magazine and ran next door to my grandma's house. I hesitantly asked her, "Could we maybe...make this cheesecake...sometime?" She enthusiastically responded, "Let's make it right now!" For a girl who couldn't get enough of baking, this is one of my favorite memories of Grandma Wilken and a great example of her vibrancy and love for her grandkids.*

ACTIVE TIME: 35 minutes | **TOTAL TIME:** 5 hours 35 minutes | **YIELD:** 8 servings

INGREDIENTS

Compote:

- 1⅓ cups blueberries, fresh or frozen
- 3 tablespoons sugar
- 1 tablespoon lemon juice
- 1 tablespoon water
- 2 teaspoons cornstarch

Crust:

- 1½ cups graham cracker crumbs
- ½ cup salted butter, melted
- 2 tablespoons sugar
- ¼ teaspoon salt

Filling:

- 2 (8 oz.) packages cream cheese, softened
- 1 cup sugar
- 2 large eggs
- 1 teaspoon vanilla extract

DIRECTIONS

[1] *Prepare the compote.* Cook the blueberries and sugar in a small saucepan over medium heat until hot and bubbly and you can see a few blueberries have burst. (If you are using frozen blueberries, start the heat on low until they are thawed and then increase it to medium.) Whisk lemon juice, water, and cornstarch in a small bowl. Stir the cornstarch slurry into the blueberries. Cook for another 1 to 2 minutes until thick. Pour onto a heatproof dinner plate and spread in a single layer. Refrigerate until the compote is no longer hot (it can still be a bit warm, just not piping hot).

[2] *Next, prepare the crust.* Toss the graham cracker crumbs, butter, sugar, and salt in a medium-size mixing bowl until evenly coated. Press the crumbs into a 9-inch pie pan, using a measuring cup to press the crust up the sides. Refrigerate the crust while you prepare the filling.

[3] *Now, get ready to bake.* Preheat the oven to 350 degrees.

[4] In a stand mixer fitted with a paddle attachment, cream the cream cheese until smooth. Keep the mixer on a low speed the entire time. Beating on a high speed will incorporate air into the batter and can cause your cheesecake to crack. Add sugar and beat until smooth. Add eggs and vanilla and mix until combined. Pour the filling into the prepared crust.

[5] Spoon teaspoonfuls of blueberry compote over the filling. Swirl the compote into the batter using a butter knife.

[6] Bake for 30 to 35 minutes. Give the cheesecake a gentle wiggle. If the edges are set but the center is a bit wobbly, it is ready to come out. Allow it to cool until you can handle it, then transfer it to the refrigerator until chilled (about 4 hours or overnight). Serve. Store leftovers in the fridge.

Rhubarb Custard Crumb Cake

Grandma Pearl is well-known for her rhubarb custard pie. This recipe keeps all of the yummy flavors of zingy rhubarb and creamy custard but swaps the pie crust for a vanilla cake with a crumble topping. This cake can be served midmorning with a cup of coffee or after supper with a scoop of vanilla ice cream.

ACTIVE TIME: 35 minutes | **TOTAL TIME:** 2 hours 15 minutes | **YIELD:** 9 squares

INGREDIENTS

Custard:

- 1 cup whole milk
- 2 large egg yolks
- ¼ cup sugar
- 1½ tablespoons cornstarch
- Pinch of salt
- 1 tablespoon salted butter
- ½ teaspoon vanilla extract

Batter:

- 1⅓ cups sugar
- 1 cup + 1 tablespoon all-purpose flour
- 3 tablespoons cornstarch
- 1¼ teaspoons baking powder
- ⅛ teaspoon baking soda
- ¼ teaspoon salt
- ½ cup salted butter, softened and cut into about 6 chunks
- 1 large egg
- 1 large egg yolk
- ½ cup sour cream
- ¼ cup whole milk
- 1 teaspoon vanilla extract
- 1½ cups diced rhubarb

DIRECTIONS

[1] *First, prepare the custard.* Heat the milk in the microwave for 1 minute or until hot and steamy.

[2] While the milk is heating, whisk the egg yolks, sugar, cornstarch, and salt until smooth.

[3] Slowly stream in hot milk, constantly whisking to temper the eggs. Whisk until thoroughly combined. Pour back into the microwave-safe dish and microwave for 1 minute. If it is not yet the consistency of pudding, continue microwaving it for 1-minute increments, stirring in between. Add butter and vanilla. Let sit until butter is melted, then whisk until smooth. Pour it onto a dinner plate in a thin layer (this helps speed up the cooling process). Cover with plastic wrap, pressing the wrap to the surface of the custard. Refrigerate until chilled, about 25 minutes.

[4] *Now, prepare the cake batter.* Preheat the oven to 350 degrees.

[5] Mix the sugar, flour, cornstarch, baking powder, baking soda, and salt in a stand mixer fitted with a paddle attachment on low speed until combined. Add the chunks of butter and stir until the mixture looks like wet sand. Remove ⅔ cup of the crumbs for the topping and set aside.

[6] Add the egg, egg yolk, sour cream, milk, and vanilla and stir until just combined. Add the rhubarb and stir until combined.

[7] *Let's put it all together.* Pour the batter into a greased and parchment-lined 9-inch square pan. Drop tablespoon-size dollops of the custard over the batter and gently swirl the custard into the batter using a butter knife. Sprinkle the reserved crumble over the top. Bake for 50 to 55 minutes until golden brown and set. Allow it to cool. Cut into squares and serve. Store leftovers in the refrigerator.

Throw Together an Easy Montage Video

I will never forget the Mother's Day we came home from church, opened up the pizzas we picked up in town, hooked a phone up to the projector, and pushed play. Rewind about 12 hours before that, I had just gone to bed when I realized I had nothing to give my mom for Mother's Day, and the idea of making a special video popped into my head. Needless to say, my mom loved it and it's still something we watch to this day.

Creating a video to celebrate someone special who has made an impact on your life is the perfect gift. It doesn't add clutter but is something you enjoy with the recipient the first time you share it, and they can appreciate it again and again. This is a great gift to give parents, grandparents, teachers, aunts, uncles—really any of your "village people."

I'm not going to break down apps and software because these can change, but I would encourage you to use a smartphone and the simple editing software that comes with it. If you get stuck, there are typically how-to videos for each software. You can create two different types of videos: a slideshow and an interview-style video.

Slideshow

First, compile pictures of your honoree. If you already have a collection of photos on your phone or computer, this is super simple. Our family has most of our older photos in albums, and for that I recommend finding some good natural lighting and simply snapping pictures of the pictures. You can scan them for a little better quality, but for me, it's about finishing the project and not getting too caught up in the details. Or head to Facebook or Instagram to download pictures of them there. This is probably fairly obvious, but I will say that you are looking for pictures of them making an impact—so when I was making this for mom for Mother's Day, I was looking for pictures of my mom with her kids through the years.

Interview

This takes the video to the next level by involving the people on who your honoree has made an impact. So for Mother's Day, that's her kids. If you live near all the people in your video, get together for a quick shoot and set up your smartphone on a tripod or a stack of books in front of an undistracting background. Or if you're too spread out, get the word out and have people film their own videos and send them to you. If you have people make their own video, specify whether you want them horizontal or vertical. Pick 3 to 5 questions, some with one-word answers and some with long answers. You can come up with your own questions, but here are some of the ones I have used before:

1. Describe your mom in one word.
2. What is your favorite thing to do with your mom?
3. Who would play your mom if they were to make a movie about her?
4. What is your favorite memory of your mom?
5. If your mom was an ice cream flavor, what would she be? Why?

Prompt people to speak in complete sentences. For example, "If I were to describe my mom in one word, it would be..." If you don't do this, no one will know what you are talking about.

Then, add the videos to your smartphone video editor and group the questions together. For example, add all of question 1 videos back-to-back, then question 2, and so on.

There, you have a meaningful gift that doesn't add to the clutter but is something they can enjoy year after year!

Celebrate the Memory of Someone Special

A hard reality of having a beautiful village of people invested in your life is loss. This might seem dark and painful—almost like it doesn't fit in a book about celebration. But I believe we can and should celebrate the people who have impacted our lives even if they are no longer with us. Just because someone passes away doesn't mean that their impact on our lives dies with them. It is often the opposite—with a loss, we are often reminded of the effect these people have had on our lives. Not only can we celebrate their impact, but we can also thank God for their place in our lives. If you want to honor the memory of someone in a meaningful way, I encourage you to focus on four main things: simplicity, community, impact, and timing.

Simplicity

It doesn't have to be complicated. We honored my late papa one Christmas by lighting a candle at the dinner table to remember him. It can be as simple as lighting a candle, saying a few things, thanking God for this person, or sharing a meal they enjoyed. You don't need to organize a massive event to honor your loved one.

A few months after my grandad passed away, his birthday rolled around. We gathered at his house and made his favorite meal: salad, steak, baked potatoes, and angel food cake with strawberries. It wasn't complicated, but it was a special time to connect and remember him together.

Community

Choosing a day like their birthday or a holiday takes what could be a hard day to walk through alone and brings family and friends together to support each other. You can also bring more people in by blessing the people who were important to your loved one. My grandma Lulu Mae was born on May 1st, or May Day. When

I was a little girl, she would help us make May Day baskets to celebrate. A few years after my grandma passed away, my parents, siblings, aunt, uncle, and cousins got together and continued the tradition. We baked cookies, arranged flowers, and put the baskets together before splitting them up and heading out. We chose to take the baskets to people who were special to my grandma. As we dropped the May Day baskets off in honor of my grandma, people were blessed by the gesture, and we were able to visit about her with her nieces, nephews, and friends.

Impact

Using this as an opportunity to impact other people not only honors the memory of one you lost, but it also takes heartache and gives it action. We made May Day baskets to honor my grandma, but you could whip up a few batches of your loved one's favorite treat and deliver them to people who were special to them.

Timing

There shouldn't be pressure about the timing. You can celebrate soon after losing a loved one or ten years later. It can be an annual tradition or whenever you desire. Don't put a lot of pressure on it.

These are simply some ideas to start with. These special people have made such a unique and significant impact on us, and there are so many ways to honor their memory and celebrate their impact. If they had a love of horses, it could be going on a trail ride with your whole family, or if they were a quilting fanatic, piece a quilt together, or if they were a baker, make their favorite recipes together. Use these ideas as inspiration to honor the memory of someone special to you.

CHAPTER 5

Major Milestones

[SHOWSTOPPING DESSERTS]

Maybe it's just the teacher in me, but I really love any type of milestone celebration—graduation, retirement, milestone anniversary or birthday, whatever! I am a little embarrassed to say that when I started my master's degree, I did think about traveling across the country, walking across the stage, and how exciting it would feel. While walking across a stage or being recognized by your company can be very satisfying, the joy really is in the people who were alongside you.

These mountaintop moments are meaningful and should be recognized in a significant way. It is a culmination of the hundreds and sometimes thousands of days this person has put in the work. They reflect big accomplishments and all of the little moments between good and bad—stressful days, lighthearted banter, sad times, inside jokes, hard decisions, and small victories. It takes an enormous amount of work and many days of putting one foot in front of the other to get to the momentous occasions. There are many obstacles to overcome in the journey to reach this high point. Ultimately, these celebrations point to God's faithfulness. He gives us the strength for each day.

A landmark occasion calls for an impressive dessert, so in this chapter, we're making show-stopping desserts that are big, beautiful, and make a visual impact! While these desserts make a statement, they maintain the "doability factor."

Not So Extreme Oreo Cheesecake

In my last semester of college, I lived five minutes from a Cheesecake Factory—this is a very dangerous location. I always had a love-hate relationship with it because it was so yummy (obviously), but the pieces were ginormous, and I never felt great after stopping there. So this recipe is inspired by my favorite cheesecake flavor—Oreo Dream Extreme Cheesecake, with less richness and much smaller pieces. The layers are not exactly the same as the original, but you'll never notice the difference. This cheesecake stands tall layered with a brownie base, Oreo cheesecake, Oreo mousse, chocolate whipped cream, and finished with a dusting of Oreo crumbs. Even though these pieces are smaller than the Cheesecake Factory version, I think you could go even smaller if you're serving a bigger crowd.

ACTIVE TIME: 1 hour | **TOTAL TIME:** 7 hours 45 minutes | **YIELD:** 12 servings (2 × 4 inches)

INGREDIENTS

- 1 (19 oz.) pkg. brownie mix and ingredients called for on the package

Cheesecake:

- 3 (8 oz.) pkgs. cream cheese, softened
- ¾ cup sugar
- 3 large eggs
- 2 teaspoons vanilla extract
- 24 Oreos

Mousse:

- 1½ cups heavy whipping cream
- ½ cup powdered sugar
- 2 tablespoons instant vanilla pudding mix
- 8 Oreos, crushed

Topping:

- Chocolate Whipped Cream (page 215)
- Chocolate syrup (optional)
- 3 Oreos

DIRECTIONS

[1] Preheat the oven to 350 degrees.

[2] *Parbake the brownie base.* Prepare the brownie batter according to the package directions. Pour it into a greased and parchment-lined 9 × 13-inch pan. Bake for 15 minutes.

[3] *Add the cheesecake layer on top.* While the brownies bake, beat the cream cheese in a stand mixer fitted with the paddle attachment on low speed until no lumps remain. Add the sugar and beat until smooth. Add the eggs and vanilla and mix until combined.

[4] Pour the cheesecake batter over the parbaked crust. Arrange the 24 Oreos in a single layer over the batter and press them down in the batter. Use an offset spatula to smooth the cheesecake over the Oreos. The cookies should be covered by the cheesecake. Bake for 25 to 30 minutes or until set. Allow the cheesecake to cool until you can handle it, then transfer it to the refrigerator until chilled (about 1 to 2 hours).

[5] *Next add the Oreo mousse.* Whip the heavy cream, powdered sugar, and pudding mix in a stand mixer fitted with the whisk attachment on medium speed until soft peaks form. Add the Oreo crumbs and whip until the Oreos are distributed throughout. Dump the mousse onto the cheesecake and spread it into an even layer using an offset spatula. Refrigerate for at least 2 hours to allow the Oreos to soften and the mousse to set up. Transfer the cheesecake to the freezer 30 minutes before serving to help achieve cleaner cuts.

[6] *Prep the finishing touches and plate each dessert.* Prepare the Chocolate Whipped Cream according to the recipe directions. Transfer it to a piping bag fitted with a large round tip.

[7] Set out 12 dessert plates and swirl chocolate syrup, if using, in a circular pattern on each plate.

[8] Using the parchment, lift the cheesecake out of the pan. Dip a sharp chef's knife into hot water and cut it into slices. Wipe the blade with a paper towel between cuts. Place each slice on a plate. Pipe chocolate whipped cream onto each cheesecake square. I like to pipe mine in a zig zag.

[9] Open and scrape the cream from 3 Oreos and discard the cream. Place the cookies in a freezer bag and use a rolling pin to very finely crush the Oreos. Use a sieve to sprinkle the Oreo dust over each cake slice. Serve. Store leftovers in the refrigerator.

Fancy Cake

This cake is inspired by the classic opera cake. It's similar to a tiramisu with coffee and chocolate but with a few differences. This cake uses an almond sponge instead of ladyfingers, a sweetened coffee syrup in place of straight espresso, a coffee buttercream instead of mascarpone cream, and also adds thin layers of rich ganache. The thin layers produce a cake that is impressive to look at with a chocolate-forward flavor profile. This cake is great to make a day or two in advance. Cut the slices just before serving so the cake doesn't dry out.

ACTIVE TIME: 45 minutes | **TOTAL TIME:** 3 hours 35 minutes | **YIELD:** 8 squares

INGREDIENTS

Ganache:

- 1 cup heavy whipping cream
- 1½ cups semisweet chocolate chips

Cake:

- 4 large egg whites
- 3 tablespoons sugar
- 5 large eggs
- 1½ cups almond flour
- 1 cup powdered sugar
- ⅓ cup all-purpose flour
- 4 tablespoons salted butter, melted

Syrup:

- ⅓ cup boiling water
- ⅓ cup sugar
- 1 tablespoon instant coffee

Buttercream:

- 1 tablespoon hot water
- 2 tablespoons instant coffee
- 1 cup salted butter, softened
- 2 cups powdered sugar
- ¼ teaspoon salt

DIRECTIONS

[1] *First make the ganache.* In a microwave-safe bowl, heat the heavy cream and chocolate chips in 30-second increments, stirring in between, until all of the chocolate is melted, about 2 minutes. Allow to cool completely.

[2] *Then, make the cake.* Heat the oven to 425 degrees. Add the egg whites and 3 tablespoons sugar to a stand mixer fitted with a whisk attachment. Whisk on low speed, slowly increasing the speed every minute until stiff peaks form, about 5 minutes. Transfer the egg whites to a separate mixing bowl.

[3] In the now empty stand mixer bowl, beat the eggs on medium speed until foamy. Add the almond flour and powdered sugar and beat until thick and fluffy, about 3 minutes.

[4] Add the all-purpose flour and stir until combined. Add the whipped egg whites and beat at medium speed until almost combined and a few streaks of egg whites remain.

[5] Add the melted butter and stir until just combined. Using an offset spatula, spread the batter onto a greased and parchment-lined rimmed 13 × 18-inch baking sheet and bake for 7 to 10 minutes, or until the cake springs back when lightly pressed. Cool completely.

[6] Use a butter knife to loosen the edges of the cake from the pan. Remove the cake from the pan and use a serrated knife to trim ¼ inch off of each side, discarding the edges. Cut the remaining rectangle in half one way and then the other way to create 4 rectangles.

[7] *Next, make the coffee syrup.* In a heat-safe dish, stir boiling water, sugar, and instant coffee until everything is dissolved.

[8] *After that, make the buttercream.* Mix hot water and instant coffee until the coffee is dissolved. This is the coffee concentrate for the buttercream.

[9] In a clean stand mixer bowl fitted with a paddle attachment, beat the butter, powdered sugar, and salt until no lumps remain. Add the coffee concentrate (not the syrup, but the concentrate!) and stir until incorporated.

[10] *Now assemble the cake.* Place one cake rectangle on a baking sheet. Use a pastry brush to soak it generously with the coffee syrup. Scoop about one-fourth of the coffee buttercream on top and spread it into a thin layer with an offset spatula. Pour about one-fourth of the ganache over the buttercream and spread using an offset spatula. Repeat three more times. Refrigerate for at least 2 hours.

[11] Using a knife dipped in hot water, trim about ¼ inch off the edges of the cake, wiping the knife clean between each cut. Cut the remaining cake into 8 squares. Serve. Store leftovers in the fridge.

Paris-Brest

Looking to make a big impact? This is the dessert for the job! The giant pastry ring looks fancy and labor-intensive but comes together lickety-split. The trickiest part of the process is letting the ring bake long enough. It will puff and be golden in the first 15 to 20 minutes, but if you pull it out early, it will be too wet inside and collapse. Pâte à Choux rises because of all of the steam created by a very wet dough, and if you open the door too early, you release the steam and risk it falling. So leave it unbothered for the full bake time before checking on it.

ACTIVE TIME: 40 minutes | **TOTAL TIME:** 2 hours 40 minutes | **YIELD:** 8–12 servings

INGREDIENTS

- Pâte à Choux (page 217)
- 1 large egg, beaten

Filling:

- ½ cup chocolate hazelnut spread
- 1 (8 oz.) pkg. cream cheese, softened
- 1¾ cups powdered sugar, plus more for sifting
- ½ cup unsweetened cocoa powder
- 2 teaspoons vanilla extract
- 2 cups heavy whipping cream

DIRECTIONS

[1] Preheat the oven to 425 degrees.

[2] Prepare the Pâte à Choux according to recipe directions and transfer the batter to a piping bag.

[3] Trace an 8-inch circle using a pencil onto a piece of parchment paper. Flip the paper over (pencil side down) and place it onto a 13 × 18-inch rimmed baking sheet.

[4] Snip a large corner off the bag. Pipe over the circle that you traced. Continue piping circles, one on top of the other building up the pastry until the piping bag is empty. Blend the different circles using the tines of a fork to create grooves over the top of the pastry.

[5] Brush the exterior of the pastry with the egg. Bake for 10 minutes. Don't open the oven door. Reduce the temperature to 375 and bake for an additional 40 to 50 minutes or until deep golden and dry. Turn the oven off and open the door a few inches. Allow it to cool completely.

[6] Use a bread knife to cut the ring in half horizontally. Remove the top half. Use your fingers to scoop out any of the wet webbing inside. Use the back of a spoon to smear the chocolate hazelnut spread inside the bottom half.

[7] Beat cream cheese, powdered sugar, cocoa powder, vanilla, and ½ cup heavy cream in a stand mixer fitted with the paddle attachment until smooth and no lumps remain, scraping down the bowl occasionally. Add the rest of the heavy cream and beat until smooth. Swap in the whisk attachment for the paddle attachment and whip until thick. Transfer the cream to a piping bag fitted with a large star tip. Pipe swirls of the cream over the chocolate hazelnut spread. Replace the top half of the pastry. Sift powdered sugar over the top. Cut into pieces and serve. Store leftovers in the fridge.

Berry Roll Cake

If you've never made a roll cake, this is the perfect beginner-friendly option. An angel food cake mix not only speeds up the process but also makes rolling effortless, as this spongy cake is sturdy without being prone to cracking. The whipped cream cheese filling holds it together, and the berries brighten up the look and the flavor profile.

ACTIVE TIME: 40 minutes | **TOTAL TIME:** 2 hours | **YIELD:** 8–12 servings

INGREDIENTS

- 1 (16 oz.) pkg. angel food cake mix
- Powdered sugar for dusting
- 1 (8 oz.) pkg. cream cheese, softened
- 1 cup powdered sugar
- 2 teaspoons vanilla extract
- 1 cup heavy whipping cream
- 1 cup diced fresh strawberries
- 1 cup fresh blueberries
- 1 cup fresh raspberries
- Extra powdered sugar for dusting

DIRECTIONS

[1] Preheat the oven to 400 degrees.

[2] Prepare angel food cake mix according to package directions.

[3] Pour the batter onto a parchment-lined 13 × 18-inch rimmed baking sheet. Bake for about 20 to 22 minutes or until it springs back when gently pressed and is golden brown. Use a butter knife to gently go around the pan, loosening the cake from the pan.

[4] Spread a tea towel out and use a sieve to dust it with a light coating of powdered sugar. Flip the still-hot cake out of the pan onto the tea towel with the short side nearest you. Also, leave a few inches of the towel showing on the side nearest you. Remove the pan and slowly peel off the parchment paper. Flip the bit of towel over the edge of the cake. Use your hands to slowly roll the towel and the cake up tightly. Let it cool completely, about an hour.

[5] Beat cream cheese on low speed until smooth in a stand mixer fitted with the paddle attachment. Add powdered sugar and vanilla and mix until combined. Add the heavy cream and mix until smooth. Swap the paddle attachment for the whisk and whip until stiff peaks form. Reserve about ⅓ cup of the whipped mixture.

[6] Toss strawberries, blueberries, and raspberries in a small bowl. Reserve about ⅓ cup of the berries.

[7] Gently unroll the cake. Spread the filling in an even layer over the cake using an offset spatula. Sprinkle the berries over the cream and gently press down.

[8] Roll up gently. Spread the reserved cream mixture down the middle of the top of the cake about 2 inches wide, pressing the reserved berries into the cream. Sift powdered sugar over the top to finish. Serve. Store leftovers in the fridge.

Peanut Butter S'mores Baked Alaska

She's definitely a stunner. But if you glance down at the recipe list, you'll be pleasantly surprised because it's pretty slim. The base is made using a boxed brownie mix and a graham cracker crust. You then mound ice cream on top and smother the whole thing in light, fluffy meringue. You can toast it using a torch or simply set your oven to broil to get that lovely golden crispy meringue. Be careful when you are toasting in the oven, as the top can burn quickly.

ACTIVE TIME: 30 minutes | **TOTAL TIME:** 8 hours 40 minutes | **YIELD:** 8–12 servings

INGREDIENTS

- 1 (19 oz.) pkg. brownie mix and ingredients called for on the package
- ½ cup salted butter, melted
- 1 cup graham cracker crumbs
- 1½ quarts chocolate peanut butter ice cream, softened
- Sit Back and Relax Meringue (page 217)

DIRECTIONS

[1] Preheat the oven to 325 degrees.

[2] Prepare the brownie batter according to the package directions; set aside.

[3] Toss together the melted butter and graham cracker crumbs in a small bowl.

[4] Dump the graham cracker crumbs into a greased and parchment-lined 8-inch round cake pan. Use the bottom of a measuring cup to press the crumbs into an even layer.

[5] Pour brownie batter over the top and bake for 40 to 45 minutes or until set. Allow it to cool to room temperature. Run a knife around the edge and freeze for 30 minutes.

[6] Line a 1½-quart bowl with plastic wrap, leaving extra plastic wrap hanging over the edge. Transfer the ice cream to the lined bowl. Fold the excess plastic wrap back over the ice cream, and use your hand to press down firmly on it so that there are no air pockets. Freeze for 1 hour.

[7] Remove the ice cream and brownies from the freezer. Remove the brownie base from the pan and place it graham crust side down on your serving plate if you plan to use a torch or on a baking sheet if you plan to broil it in the oven. Unmold the ice cream from the bowl and remove all the plastic wrap. Stack the ice cream mound with the flat side on the brownie base. Freeze for 2 hours.

[8] Prepare the Sit Back and Relax Meringue according to recipe directions.

[9] Plop a generous mound of meringue on top of the ice cream. Use an offset spatula to spread the meringue over the top and sides. Be sure to cover the ice cream entirely, as the meringue acts as insulation from the heat. Freeze. If toasting with a torch, freeze for at least 1 to 2 hours, but if broiling in the oven, freeze for 3 hours or overnight.

BROILER DIRECTIONS: Set the oven to broil. Place the baked Alaska about 12 inches from the heating element at the top of the oven. Brown for 2 to 3 minutes. Keep a very close eye on it, as it will turn from golden to burned very quickly and each oven is different. Use a large metal spatula to carefully transfer the dessert to your serving dish. Serve immediately. Store leftovers in the freezer.

TORCH DIRECTIONS: Use a large metal spatula to carefully transfer the dessert to your serving dish. Brown the outside of the meringue with a torch, holding it about 6 inches away. Move in circular motions to brown the surface of the meringue. Cut into slices. Store leftovers in the freezer.

Grand Chocolate Towers

Ranchers tend not to go on vacation, and if they do they don't usually go very far, which is why our family has taken many of our vacations in the Black Hills of South Dakota—but I'm not complaining. Besides all of the gorgeous scenery and biking trails, it's also home to one of our favorite restaurants—the Alpine Inn. It's a German Bavarian–style restaurant with a huge dessert menu, and after trying many of their desserts, my go-to is the Grand Chocolate Tower. This stately dessert features chocolate mousse layered with chewy brownies topped with whipped cream and served with an extra-long spoon. And if it's your birthday you get a sparkler on top of your tower, and since this chapter is all about "showstopping desserts" I figured the sparklers wouldn't hurt anything.

ACTIVE TIME: 45 minutes | **TOTAL TIME:** 1 hour 45 minutes | **YIELD:** 6 parfaits

INGREDIENTS

- 1 (19 oz.) pkg. brownie mix and ingredients called for on the package
- Chocolate Whipped Cream (page 215)
- Fudge Sauce (page 211)
- 1 cup heavy whipping cream
- ½ cup powdered sugar
- ½ teaspoon vanilla extract

DIRECTIONS

[1] Prepare and bake the brownies according to the directions in an 8-inch greased and parchment-lined pan. Cool completely. Chill in the fridge.

[2] Prepare the Chocolate Whipped Cream according to the recipe directions. Transfer it to a piping bag.

[3] Prepare the Fudge Sauce according to the recipe directions. Allow to cool to room temperature.

[4] Remove the brownie from the pan and use a chef's knife or bench scraper to chop brownies into about 1-inch square pieces.

[5] Layer the brownies, chocolate whipped cream, and fudge sauce to assemble the towers in six 8-ounce serving glasses.

[6] Whip the heavy cream, powdered sugar, and vanilla in a stand mixer fitted with a whisk attachment until medium peaks form. Transfer to a piping bag fitted with a large star tip.

[7] Pipe tall swirls of whipped cream on top of each parfait. If desired, stick a food-safe sparkler in the middle of each dessert. Light and serve. Store leftovers in the fridge.

White Chocolate Mocha Toffee Trifle

My aunt Lisa is known for her trifles. In fact, she gave each of her nieces a trifle bowl when they graduated from high school. If you don't have a trifle bowl, use any large clear bowl (that will hold at least 3 quarts) to show off the pretty layers of this dessert. This recipe is based on one of her most common creations with a few tweaks—a little more coffee flavor and fresh whipped cream instead of "whipped topping." My uncle Wade always says "trifle" is a bad name for this dessert because the word "trifle" means small or insignificant, and this dessert is anything but.

ACTIVE TIME: 40 minutes | **TOTAL TIME:** 1 hour 40 minutes | **YIELD:** 12–16 servings

INGREDIENTS

- 1 (19 oz.) pkg. brownie mix
- 3 cups heavy whipping cream
- ½ cup powdered sugar
- 1 teaspoon vanilla extract
- 2 tablespoons warm water
- 2 tablespoons instant coffee
- 2 cups cold whole milk
- 2 (3.4 oz.) pkgs. instant white chocolate pudding mix
- 4 (1.4 oz) chocolate-covered toffee bars

DIRECTIONS

[1] Prepare and bake the brownies according to the package directions for a cake-like brownie in an 8-inch greased and parchment-lined pan. Cool completely; you can pop it in the fridge to speed it up.

[2] Remove the brownie from the pan and use a chef's knife or bench scraper to chop brownies into about 1-inch square pieces.

[3] Whip the heavy cream, powdered sugar, and vanilla in a stand mixer fitted with the whisk attachment until medium peaks form.

[4] To make your white mocha mousse layer, first make a coffee concentrate by stirring the warm water and instant coffee in a small dish until the coffee is dissolved.

[5] Whisk the milk, pudding mixes, and coffee concentrate in a medium-size mixing bowl for a couple of minutes until smooth and thick. Add 2 cups of whipped cream and gently stir until no streaks remain.

[6] Chop the toffee bars using a chef's knife into about ¼-inch chunks.

[7] Spread one-third of the brownie chunks in the bottom of a 3-quart trifle bowl. Spoon one-third of the white mocha mousse and use a spatula to spread it in an even layer. Spoon one third of the whipped cream and use a spatula to spread it in an even layer. Sprinkle one-third of the chopped toffee bars. Repeat two more times. Store in the refrigerator until ready to serve. Store leftovers in the fridge.

Pineapple Puff Pastry Tart

As a kid, pineapple was considered a special treat, and our family would only eat it a few times a year, so this pineapple tart feels festive to me. Despite the fancy appearance, the crust is made using store-bought puff pastry, and the pineapple curd cooks up in four minutes in the microwave using canned pineapple juice. To keep the flavors fresh, I mix the cooked curd with fresh pineapple to brighten the flavors, and the whipped cream on top is a no-brainer. If you are in a rush or want to keep things simple, spread the whipped cream over the top and skip the piping bag.

ACTIVE TIME: 35 minutes | **TOTAL TIME:** 3 hours 15 minutes | **YIELD:** 9 servings

INGREDIENTS

Pineapple Curd Filling:

- 1 cup canned pineapple juice
- 1 tablespoon cornstarch
- ½ cup salted butter, melted and slightly cooled
- ½ cup sugar
- 5 large egg yolks
- 1 cup finely diced fresh pineapple

Crust:

- 1 sheet puff pastry (½ of a 17.3 oz. pkg.), thawed
- 1 large egg

Whipped Cream:

- 1½ cups heavy whipping cream
- ½ cup powdered sugar
- 1 teaspoon vanilla extract

DIRECTIONS

[1] *First, make the pineapple curd.* Whisk the pineapple juice and cornstarch in a small bowl until no lumps remain.

[2] Whisk melted butter, sugar, egg yolks, and the cornstarch slurry until smooth. Microwave for 1 minute. Stir and repeat microwaving for 1-minute intervals, stirring in between until it reaches the consistency of gravy.

[3] Transfer the curd to a storage container and press plastic wrap to the surface. Chill for 2 hours or until chilled and thick.

[4] *Then prepare your pastry.* Preheat the oven to 400 degrees.

[5] Unfold the sheet of puff pastry onto a large piece of parchment. Roll the dough gently to smooth out the folds, resulting in a 9 × 9-inch square. Use a paring knife to score (without cutting all the way through) a 1-inch border around the outside. I like to use the edge of a cutting board as a straight edge to guide my knife. Use a fork to poke inside the scored rectangle. Whisk the egg in a small bowl and brush over the 1-inch border around the tart.

[6] Bake for 15 to 18 minutes or until golden brown. Use a metal spatula to press down the pricked rectangle, leaving a border around the edge. Cool completely.

[7] *Let's put it all together.* Mix the thickened curd and fresh pineapple pieces. Dump it into the center of the puff pastry crust and spread it into an even layer using a spatula.

[8] Whip heavy cream, powdered sugar, and vanilla in a stand mixer fitted with a whisk attachment until medium peaks form. Transfer to a piping bag fitted with a large star tip. Pipe swirls of whipped cream over the pineapple filling. Cut into squares and serve. Store leftovers in the refrigerator.

Raspberry Crusted Pound Cake

Each night at summer camp, we would go to a different country for supper. One night we had "Australian" food. I don't know how authentic it really was, as I remember having the combination of pound cake, chocolate whipped cream, and fresh raspberries. It was delicious. But in all of my googling, I have not found a connection to Australia. Regardless, it's delicious, and this raspberry-covered cake looks impressive, but it is an effortless no-bake dessert that starts with a store-bought pound cake. I pick up the pound cake from the freezer section. Each bite features a rich chocolate cream, dense pound cake, and tart raspberries.

ACTIVE TIME: 25 minutes | **TOTAL TIME:** 25 minutes | **YIELD:** 8–10 servings

INGREDIENTS

- 24 oz. fresh raspberries
- 1 (16 oz.) pound cake
- Chocolate Whipped Cream (page 215)

DIRECTIONS

[1] Rinse raspberries in cold water and place them on layers of paper towels to dry off.

[2] Cut the pound cake in half horizontally. Place bottom half of the cake on your desired serving dish. Spoon about ⅔ cup of Chocolate Whipped Cream on top and spread in an even layer using an offset spatula.

[3] Replace the top half gently, pressing down until the top of the cake is level. Frost the sides and top of the cake with the chocolate whipped cream.

[4] Press the raspberries into the sides and top of the cake, packing them in a tight formation. Refrigerate until ready to serve. Store leftovers in the fridge.

Scotcheroo Bundt

The humble but delicious scotcheroo gets a "glow-up" in this bundt form. It's the same Midwest scotcheroo you know and love packed into a bundt pan and topped with a luscious chocolate peanut butter glaze. If you're looking for a no-bake dessert with all the visual impact of a traditional cake, this one's for you.

ACTIVE TIME: 25 minutes | **TOTAL TIME:** 1 hour 25 minutes | **YIELD:** 16–20 servings

INGREDIENTS

Cake:

- 2 cups light corn syrup
- 2 cups sugar
- 2 cups creamy peanut butter
- 12 cups puffed rice cereal or Rice Krispies (12 oz. box)

Topping:

- ½ cup semisweet chocolate chips
- ½ cup creamy peanut butter
- 1 tablespoon salted butter

DIRECTIONS

[1] *First, make the cake layer.* Stir the corn syrup and sugar in a large microwave-safe dish and heat for 3 minutes. Stir. If the sugar is not dissolved, microwave for another minute. Add the peanut butter and stir until smooth. Add the cereal and stir until all of the cereal is coated.

[2] Very generously grease a 12-cup bundt cake pan. Add half of the cereal mixture and press it firmly into the pan. Scoop the rest of the cereal into the pan and press until the top is flat. Adding it in two batches helps make sure the cereal gets into all the crevices. Allow to cool completely, about 1 to 2 hours.

[3] With a knife, go around the edge of the pan to loosen the "cake." Invert the bundt cake onto your desired serving dish.

[4] *Prepare the topping.* Microwave chocolate chips, peanut butter, and butter in a medium-size microwave-safe bowl for 30 seconds. Stir. Microwave for another 15 seconds and stir. Repeat until no lumps remain.

[5] Pour the chocolate mixture over the top of the cake. Jiggle the plate to encourage the chocolate to run down the sides. Let sit until the chocolate is set. Store leftovers in airtight container.

Raspberry Almond Cupcakes

I didn't think that there would be any cupcake recipes in this cookbook. Truthfully, I've gotten kind of weary over the last decade of people always wanting me to make cupcakes. It became what I was known for, so it is what people have requested over and over and over...and over. So you have to know that this cupcake is special to make the cut. First, I love this almond cake. The almond paste takes the almond flavor to the next level and creates a beautiful dense, moist texture. I wanted to develop a cupcake recipe that required zero fresh fruit, as it can be difficult to find it out of season—not to mention expensive. Frozen raspberries fit the bill in this recipe. Instead of taking the time to core and fill the cupcakes, I use the frosting to create a well to hold the filling. The filling plays double duty—not only sitting front and center in the cupcake, but also blended into the frosting to add tart raspberry flavor.

ACTIVE TIME: 45 minutes | **TOTAL TIME:** 2 hour 40 minutes | **YIELD:** 12 cupcakes

INGREDIENTS

- ¾ cup Two-Ingredient Raspberry Filling (page 213)

Cake:

- 4 oz. almond paste
- ¾ cup salted butter, softened
- ⅔ cup sugar
- 4 large eggs
- ½ teaspoon vanilla extract
- ½ cup all-purpose flour
- ½ teaspoon baking powder

Frosting:

- 4 oz. cream cheese, softened
- ¾ cup powdered sugar
- 1 cup heavy whipping cream

DIRECTIONS

[1] Prepare the Two-Ingredient Raspberry Filling according to the recipe directions. Strain using a fine mesh sieve to remove the seeds. Refrigerate until chilled and thick.

[2] Preheat the oven to 325 degrees.

[3] *It's time to make the cake.* In a stand mixer fitted with the paddle attachment, cream the almond paste, butter, and sugar on medium speed until smooth.

[4] Add the eggs one at a time, beating after each addition until thick and fluffy. Add the vanilla and mix until combined.

[5] Add the flour and baking powder and mix on low until just combined. Use a scoop to portion the batter into 12 cupcake liners. Bake for 20 to 25 minutes until golden brown and set in the center. Cool completely.

[6] *Now let's make the frosting and put it together.* In a stand mixer fitted with the paddle attachment, mix cream cheese and powdered sugar until no lumps remain. Add ½ cup raspberry filling and mix until smooth. Add the heavy cream and mix until frosting comes together, occasionally scraping the bottom and sides of the bowl. Switch out the paddle attachment for the whisk attachment. Whip on medium-high speed until thick. Transfer the frosting to a piping bag fitted with a star tip. Transfer the remaining raspberry filling to another piping bag and snip a small tip.

[7] Pipe frosting starting in the center of the cupcakes and moving outward in a spiral shape so the entire cupcake is covered with a thin layer of frosting. Then, pipe along the edge to create a dam to hold the filling. Squeeze about a teaspoon of the raspberry filling in the cavity you just created. Serve. Store leftovers in the fridge.

Host a Honey Roast

If you've never heard of a "roast," it's an American comedy sensation where the guest of honor gets made fun of in a formal setting, often by professional comedians. A roast is supposed to be fun and funny, but often they just seem mean. A honey roast has the same focus on a "guest of honor" but just sweet stuff with none of the ugly talk; hence the name honey roast. Growing up, we would often do a honey roast at home over dessert after dinner, or if we were out celebrating in a restaurant, we would do it while we waited for our food to come.

A honey roast requires no planning but creates a meaningful experience for the guest of honor. We don't do a honey roast at every party, but it's always off the cuff when we do one. If you feel like your guests need a heads-up, send a text ahead of time.

Here's how to host a honey roast...

1. Start by saying something like, "Let's do a honey roast and celebrate [insert guest of honor name here]! You can share a funny memory, a special memory, or something you appreciate about them." Often, I will repeat that list a few times, because it can take a few moments for people's brains to start going. So again, the three things are...

   Funny memory

   Special memory

   Something you appreciate about them

2. If nobody jumps in right away, you should kick off the honey roast and share something about the guest of honor to give everyone a moment to think.

3. Hopefully, people will start sharing now! Also, don't be afraid of a little quiet time; sometimes people need a few seconds to get going.

There you go: a meaningful but clutter-free way to celebrate your honoree!

Create a Surprise Retirement Memory Book

In small-town newspapers, you'll often see an announcement of a card shower for a milestone birthday or anniversary. They'll list the honoree's mailing address, and the people who know them can write them a card. This is often done for older folks who don't need anything more in the way of gifts and maybe aren't up for a big party.

I love this concept, and my cousin Monica did something similar for Aunt Linda for her retirement after 35 years of teaching public school, directing special ed, and, finally, being a college-level instructor.

In these current times, Facebook can often provide the most significant collection of people from all different points in a person's career, or maybe you can contact people from a list of emails or phone numbers. For my aunt, her list of contacts included students, coworkers, bosses, and so on.

Monica made a post that everyone but Linda could see by changing the setting before posting. Make sure to do this if you want it to be a surprise. The post basically said, "My mom is retiring! Celebrate by sending me a special memory of Mom or something that stands out to you during Linda's teaching career. Send me your message via Messenger or at my email."

I love this idea because there are so many steps to actually getting a card in the mail, but typing up a quick message takes just a minute or two. People are busy, so making it easier means more people will share! Monica then printed these messages off and put them, along with any handwritten notes and pictures, into a photo album.

BE KIND

CHAPTER 6

The Little Things

[30-MINUTE MASTERPIECES]

During a particularly busy time in my life, I started a series on my account of 30-minute recipes out of necessity. I would set a timer on my phone, film the video, and then quickly edit and post the recipe before jumping in my car and zipping to practice.

Many "30-minute" recipes may promise only 30 minutes of prep, but then need several hours in the fridge. Not these recipes. In less than 30 minutes, you will have a sweet treat ready to be enjoyed. There are many reasons to celebrate that pop up at the last minute or may seem small—like meeting a deadline at work, getting a good grade, paying off a loan, hitting a new personal best—but they are still worth celebrating!

When we live as people of celebration looking to encourage others, it has a ripple effect. Some people might say, "What's the big deal? We can't celebrate every little thing!" And that's true. We can't throw a party every day, but we do want to make people feel acknowledged and loved. Others around you will see that spirit and be encouraged to do the same. These last-minute celebrations come from a heart of gratitude.

James 1:17 starts by saying, "Every good gift and every perfect gift is from above." No good thing is a coincidence or an accident; it is a gift directly from God. When we celebrate these "little things," we are really saying, "Thank You, God!" and savoring His goodness with those around us.

Strawberry Fondue Bowls

For my cousin Moriah's high school graduation party, she had a humongous chocolate fountain along with pretzel rods, Rice Krispies Treats, strawberries, and other dippers. Wide-eyed kids and adults were drawn to it, and the first treat people dipped in the cascade of chocolate were the big, juicy strawberries. This recipe is inspired by that, but without having to clean up a monstrous machine afterward. These individual "fondue bowls" have ganache in the bottom of each bowl, so you can use a fork to eat and swirl it in the bottom of the bowl to pick up as much chocolatey goodness as possible.

ACTIVE TIME: 20 minutes | **TOTAL TIME:** 20 minutes | **YIELD:** 4 servings

INGREDIENTS

- 1 cup heavy whipping cream
- 1 cup milk chocolate chips
- 1 lb. fresh strawberries

DIRECTIONS

[1] Heat heavy cream and chocolate chips in a microwave-safe dish for 30 seconds. Stir. Repeat until no lumps remain.

[2] Pour the ganache evenly among four cereal bowls or shallow salad bowls.

[3] Hull and halve the strawberries. Arrange the strawberries over the ganache, dividing them equally across the four bowls. Serve immediately. Store leftovers in the fridge.

Salty Cracker Peanut Butter Pie

A lot of no-bake pies require several hours of chilling time before serving; not this one. Right when you finish assembling, you can cut into it. While you will get neater slices if you refrigerate for a few hours, it has enough structure to cut into it right away. The salty crust plays well with the creamy peanut butter filling, and the whipped cream helps balance the intense richness.

ACTIVE TIME: 25 minutes | **TOTAL TIME:** 25 minutes | **YIELD:** 8–10 servings

INGREDIENTS

- 2½ cups butter cracker crumbs (like Ritz or Club crackers)
- ½ cup salted butter, melted
- 2 cups heavy whipping cream
- 2¼ cups powdered sugar, divided
- 1 teaspoon vanilla extract
- 1 cup creamy peanut butter
- 1 (8 oz.) pkg. cream cheese, softened
- 1 cup chopped chocolate peanut butter cups (about 6 full-size peanut butter cups)

DIRECTIONS

[1] Toss the cracker crumbs and melted butter until the crumbs are coated and press into a 9-inch pie pan using a measuring cup to press the crust up the sides. Pop the crust in the freezer until you are ready to fill it.

[2] Whip the heavy cream, 1 cup powdered sugar, and vanilla in a stand mixer fitted with a whisk attachment until medium peaks form. Remove the whipped cream from the mixing bowl and refrigerate until ready to use.

[3] Swap in the paddle attachment for the whisk. In the same (now empty) mixing bowl, add the rest of the powdered sugar, peanut butter, and cream cheese and beat until smooth. Add half of the whipped cream and stir until combined. Dump peanut butter mousse into the crust and spread into an even layer. Spoon the remaining whipped cream on top of the mousse. Top with chopped peanut butter cups. Cut pie into slices and serve. Store leftovers in the fridge.

Lemony Fruit Pizzas

These mini fruit pizzas utilize store-bought sugar cookies to majorly speed up the prep time. The lemon flavors throughout these little pizzas inject brightness and balance out the sweetness of the grocery store cookies. Use any fresh fruit that you like to top the pizzas. I prefer simple strawberries, blueberries, and blackberries, but if you want to go '90s style, top them with grapes, canned mandarin oranges, and banana slices. One lemon will be enough to produce the juice and zest that the recipe calls for.

ACTIVE TIME: 15 minutes | **TOTAL TIME:** 15 minutes | **YIELD:** 8 servings

INGREDIENTS

- 8 store-bought sugar cookies (unfrosted)

Lemon Cream:

- 4 oz. cream cheese, softened
- ½ cup powdered sugar
- 2 teaspoons lemon juice
- 1 teaspoon lemon zest

Syrup and Topping:

- 2 teaspoons lemon juice
- 2 teaspoons powdered sugar
- About 1 cup fresh fruit (my favorites are strawberries, blueberries, and blackberries)
- Extra lemon zest

DIRECTIONS

[1] Set out your cookies on a serving tray, then prepare the lemon cream. In a small bowl, cream the cream cheese and ½ cup powdered sugar until no lumps remain. Add the lemon juice and zest and stir until combined. Spoon a scant tablespoon of lemon cream on each cookie. Use an offset spatula or a butter knife to spread the cream in an even layer.

[2] Make a syrup by whisking the lemon juice and powdered sugar until the sugar is dissolved. Toss the fruit in the syrup. Arrange the fruit on each cookie in a single layer over the cream. You can make each design the same or mix it up. Zest a bit of lemon peel over the top as a finishing touch. Serve. Store leftovers in the fridge.

Speedy Chocolate Cake

The beauty of this 30-minute cake is that the ganache frosting can be slathered on while the cake is still hot. The sprinkles add visual interest and also add a textural element. You can eat it warm or allow it to cool before serving it up. This cake is begging for generous scoops of vanilla ice cream and mugs brimming with hot coffee.

ACTIVE TIME: 10 minutes | **TOTAL TIME:** 30 minutes | **YIELD:** 18 servings (2 × 3-inch pieces)

INGREDIENTS

- Chocolate Crazy Cake batter (page 214)
- 1 cup semisweet chocolate chips
- ½ cup heavy whipping cream
- Chocolate sprinkles

DIRECTIONS

[1] Preheat the oven to 350 degrees.

[2] Prepare the Chocolate Crazy Cake Batter according to the recipe directions. Pour it into a greased and parchment-lined 9 × 13-inch pan. Bake for 15 to 18 minutes or until the cake springs back when gently pressed.

[3] While the cake is baking, mix chocolate chips and heavy cream in a medium-size bowl to make a ganache. Microwave for 30 seconds. Stir. Repeat until no lumps remain, about 2 minutes.

[4] Allow the hot cake to cool for 5 minutes. Pour the ganache over the cake and use an offset spatula to spread it in an even layer. Sprinkle a generous portion of chocolate sprinkles over the top. Cut into pieces and serve with vanilla ice cream, if desired. Store leftovers in an airtight container.

Maple Brown Sugar Whipped Coffee Float

If you've never heard of a Dalgona coffee, it is a whipped coffee made using instant coffee that was "TikTok famous" during the pandemic in 2020. In this quick ice cream treat, whipped coffee meets ice cream float meets maple flavor in a fun mashup. Coffee is such a personal preference, so if you like it not to be as strong, add more milk to adjust it to your taste, and remember that the ice cream will start to melt and dilute the strong coffee flavor. This recipe only makes two servings but can easily be scaled up to serve a crowd.

ACTIVE TIME: 5 minutes | **TOTAL TIME:** 5 minutes | **YIELD:** 2 servings

INGREDIENTS

- ¼ cup water
- 2 tablespoons instant coffee
- 2 tablespoons dark brown sugar
- ¼ teaspoon maple extract
- ½ cup whole milk
- 4 scoops vanilla ice cream (about 1½ cups)

DIRECTIONS

[1] Blend water, instant coffee, brown sugar, and maple extract with an immersion blender or a hand frother until thick and fluffy.

[2] Add the milk and blend until just combined.

[3] Scoop the ice cream into your desired serving glasses. Pour the whipped coffee over the ice cream, dividing it between the two glasses. Serve with a straw. Best enjoyed immediately.

Peaches and Cream Angel Food "Torn"ado

Truthfully, she's a bit chaotic, and she may not be the prettiest girl at the dance, but you will want her on your dance card nonetheless! Bits of angel food cake, fresh peaches, and creamy vanilla whip compose this fun, carefree dessert. Also, I love seeing ripe, juicy peach chunks in this dessert, but peaches are only succulent and juicy for a short season. Feel free to swap other fruits—blueberries, strawberries, mangos—whatever you can get your hands on! You could even use frozen fruit; just thaw it first.

ACTIVE TIME: 20 minutes | **TOTAL TIME:** 20 minutes | **YIELD:** 8–12 servings

INGREDIENTS

- 1 (14 oz.) store-bought angel food cake
- 2 cups heavy whipping cream
- 1 (14 oz.) can sweetened condensed milk
- 1 tablespoon vanilla extract
- 4 cups fresh peeled and diced peaches (about 6 medium peaches), divided

DIRECTIONS

[1] Use your hands to tear the angel food cake into bite-size pieces into a large mixing bowl.

[2] Whip the heavy cream, sweetened condensed milk, and vanilla in a stand mixer fitted with a whisk attachment until medium peaks form.

[3] Add half of the diced peaches and half the cream to the cake pieces and toss until they are coated.

[4] Transfer half of the cake mixture into a 3-quart trifle bowl. Spoon half of the remaining cream over the cake and spread it into an even layer. Arrange half of the remaining peaches over the cream. Repeat with the remaining cake, cream, and peaches. Serve. Store leftovers in the fridge.

Macerated Blackberries with Caramelized Pound Cake

This dessert takes the ordinary cake, fruit, and whipped cream combination to the next level. The pound cake gets slathered in a brown sugar and butter coating and then is toasted on the stovetop. This process adds a tasty, caramelized flavor and a nice crunch. "Macerated blackberries" sound fancy, but they are just blackberries that have been sweetened and broken down a bit. Finishing with fresh whipped cream is a given.

ACTIVE TIME: 25 minutes | **TOTAL TIME:** 25 minutes | **YIELD:** 4 servings

INGREDIENTS

- 1 store-bought pound cake

Berries:

- 1½ cups fresh blackberries
- 1 tablespoon sugar

Spread:

- ¼ cup salted butter, softened
- ¼ cup dark brown sugar
- ¼ teaspoon vanilla extract
- Pinch of salt

Whipped Cream:

- 1 cup heavy whipping cream
- ⅓ cup powdered sugar
- ½ teaspoon vanilla extract

DIRECTIONS

[1] Cut 4 slices of pound cake, making each slice about 1 inch thick (cake sizes will vary, but you may not need an entire cake). Set aside.

[2] Toss blackberries and sugar in a small bowl. Using a spoon, gently mash the blackberries to release some of their juices.

[3] Cream the butter, brown sugar, ¼ teaspoon vanilla, and salt until smooth. Spread the butter mixture over the face-up side of each of the pound cake slices.

[4] Heat a large skillet on medium heat. Place the cake slices buttered side down on the hot pan. Butter the other side of each slice that is now facing up. Cook until bubbly and brown on each side, about 3 to 4 minutes total. Keep a very close eye on the cake so that it doesn't burn. Remove the slices from the pan and allow them to cool and crisp up for 5 minutes while you make the whipped cream.

[5] Whip the heavy cream, powdered sugar, and ½ teaspoon vanilla in a stand mixer fitted with the whisk attachment until medium peaks form.

[6] Place a cake slice on each serving plate. Spoon generous dollops of whipped cream on each cake slice and top with macerated blackberries. Best enjoyed immediately.

Pistachio Faux Fried Ice Cream

Fried ice cream is impressive but can be tricky and messy, so this "faux" version is the perfect alternative. To pull off the iconic crunch of fried ice cream, you will crush cornflakes, toss with butter, sugar, salt, and cinnamon, and then toast the crumbs up in the oven. I mixed up the traditional fried ice cream components and opted for a pistachio and honey version, resulting in almost a "baklava like" flavor profile.

ACTIVE TIME: 10 minutes | **TOTAL TIME:** 30 minutes | **YIELD:** 4 servings

INGREDIENTS

- 2 cups cornflakes, crushed
- ½ cup salted butter, melted
- ¼ cup sugar
- ½ teaspoon salt
- ½ teaspoon cinnamon
- 1 pint pistachio ice cream
- Canned whipped cream
- 2 tablespoons finely chopped pistachios
- Honey for drizzling

DIRECTIONS

[1] Preheat the oven to 400 degrees.

[2] Toss crushed cornflakes, melted butter, sugar, salt, and cinnamon in a medium-size mixing bowl until crumbs are completely coated. Dump the crumbs onto a parchment-lined baking sheet and spread them into a thin layer. Bake for 8 minutes, stirring halfway through.

[3] Cool the crumbs quickly by transferring the parchment with the crumbs on it to a cool sheet pan and placing it into the freezer.

[4] While the crumbs are cooling, scoop four large balls of ice cream. Pack the ice cream into tight balls using food safe gloves or covering your hands in plastic wrap to press the ice cream together. If the ice cream gets too soft, pop it in the freezer for 5 minutes and then continue. Transfer the crumbs to a bowl. Roll each ice cream ball into the crumbs and press the crumbs into the ice cream. Place the coated balls into the freezer until ready to serve.

[5] To serve, place a fried ice cream ball on four small plates. Top with whipped cream, chopped pistachios, and a drizzle of honey. Best enjoyed immediately.

Nanaimo Bars

On a girls' trip to Banff, we stayed at a budget hotel that, truthfully, in most ways was nothing special, but every afternoon they had a dessert bar. Best hotel ever. One of the desserts they would serve was Nanaimo bars, which I later found out is a Canadian dessert. They are rich little squares with a crunchy crust, custard-like filling, and chocolate on top. This recipe is not an exact dupe but has "Nanaimo vibes." In order to get it finished up within 30 minutes, you will need to use your freezer between steps.

ACTIVE TIME: 30 minutes | **TOTAL TIME:** 30 minutes | **YIELD:** 16 (2 × 2-inch squares)

INGREDIENTS

Base:

- ¼ cup salted butter
- 1⅔ cups semisweet chocolate chips
- 2 cups crisp rice cereal
- Pinch of salt

Filling:

- ½ cup salted butter, softened
- 3 tablespoons heavy whipping cream
- 2 tablespoons instant vanilla pudding mix
- 1 teaspoon vanilla extract
- 2 cups powdered sugar

Topping:

- ½ cup semisweet chocolate chips
- 2 tablespoons butter

DIRECTIONS

[1] *First, prepare the base.* Melt butter in a medium-size bowl in the microwave for 30 seconds. Add the chocolate chips and microwave for 30 seconds. Stir. Heat for another 15 seconds and stir. If any lumps remain, continue heating the chocolate for 15-second intervals. Add the cereal and salt and stir until the cereal is completely coated. Dump the crust into a parchment-lined square pan and spread it into an even layer. If it's being stubborn, place a piece of plastic wrap over the crust and press it into a thin even layer. Freeze while you make the filling.

[2] *Next, make the filling.* Cream the butter, heavy cream, pudding mix, and vanilla in a stand mixer fitted with a paddle attachment until smooth. Add the powdered sugar and beat until incorporated. Dump onto the crust and use an offset spatula to spread the filling into an even layer. Freeze while you make the topping.

[3] *Finally, prepare the topping and assemble.* Heat chocolate chips and butter in a small bowl in the microwave for 30 seconds and stir. If any lumps remain, heat it for another 15 seconds and stir. Pour the chocolate over the filling and use an offset spatula to spread it into an even layer. Freeze for 5 minutes. Cut into squares. Serve cold. Store in the refrigerator.

Molasses Bananas Foster

This recipe is like Nebraska...it's not for everyone. I love the flavor of molasses, but if that's not your jam you'll probably want to pass on this recipe. The original bananas foster gets a makeover with the addition of molasses and ginger. Be careful not to let the syrup cook too long. We want it to be a beautiful dark caramel-colored sauce, but if cooked too long it will become hard when spooned over ice cream.

ACTIVE TIME: 15 minutes | **TOTAL TIME:** 15 minutes | **YIELD:** 4 servings

INGREDIENTS

- ⅓ cup salted butter
- ⅓ cup dark brown sugar
- ⅓ cup unsulphured molasses
- ½ teaspoon ground cinnamon
- ¼ teaspoon ground ginger
- 4 ripe but firm bananas, peeled and sliced in half lengthwise
- Vanilla ice cream

DIRECTIONS

[1] Heat butter, brown sugar, molasses, cinnamon, and ginger in a large skillet over medium heat. Stir until the butter is melted and the mixture is just combined.

[2] Place the cut side of the banana down into the syrup and use a spoon to baste the bananas by spooning the syrup over the rounded side of each banana half. Cook for 1 to 2 minutes or until the banana has softened but is not falling apart. Remove from the heat.

[3] Serve two warm banana halves with a scoop of vanilla ice cream. Spoon extra molasses sauce over the ice cream and serve. Best enjoyed immediately.

Mango Fool

Uncle Wade often tells me that a lot of the words in the dessert world make no sense. For example, a "trifle" is a huge, layered dessert, but in everyday language, the word "trifle" means "something of little importance." And while "fool" can mean "a person who acts unwisely or imprudently," it can also mean "a cold dessert made of pureed fruit mixed or served with cream or custard." The bottom line is there is definitely nothing foolish about a dessert that comes together in less than 20 minutes and features creamy mango whip and crunchy toasted coconut flakes.

ACTIVE TIME: 20 minutes | **TOTAL TIME:** 20 minutes | **YIELD:** 4 servings

INGREDIENTS

- ¼ cup coconut flakes
- 10 oz. frozen mango chunks, thawed but still cold
- ½ cup powdered sugar
- 1 cup heavy whipping cream

DIRECTIONS

[1] Toast the coconut in a small skillet over medium heat, stirring occasionally until it turns a light golden brown color, about 3 to 4 minutes. Cool completely.

[2] Blend the mango and powdered sugar using an immersion blender or in a blender until smooth. Remove ½ cup of the puree and reserve it for the top.

[3] Whip the heavy cream in a stand mixer fitted with a whisk attachment until medium peaks form. Gently stir the remaining puree into the cream until no streaks remain.

[4] Divide the mango cream among four 6-ounce serving glasses. Spoon the reserved puree over the cream. Sprinkle with the toasted coconut. Serve. Store leftovers in the fridge.

Take 5 Ice Cream Sundae Cones

One of our favorite treats that the Schwan's man would bring on his truck was the sundae cones. I took that inspiration and mixed it with one of my favorite childhood candy bars—the Take 5. This ice cream cone has all the flavors of the candy bar—pretzels, peanuts, peanut butter, caramel, and chocolate. You know how I feel about crunch, and this recipe is one for the crunch record books—you've got the crispy cone, crunchy pretzels, and salty roasted peanuts! Also, doesn't an ice cream cone just make you smile?

ACTIVE TIME: 20 minutes | **TOTAL TIME:** 30 minutes | **YIELD:** 6 ice cream cones

INGREDIENTS

- 6 waffle cones
- 1 cup semisweet chocolate chips
- ⅓ cup coconut oil
- 12 scoops of vanilla ice cream (about 6 cups)
- ⅓ cup creamy peanut butter
- 16 mini pretzel twists, coarsely crushed
- ⅓ cup roasted salted peanuts, roughly chopped
- ⅓ cup caramel sauce

DIRECTIONS

[1] Place cones in small drinking glasses on a small tray so they don't tip over while you fill them. You may need to pick the cones up to scoop ice cream into them.

[2] Make chocolate shell by microwaving chocolate chips and coconut oil in the microwave for 30 seconds. Stir and repeat until no lumps remain. Pour about 2 teaspoons of the chocolate shell into the bottom of the cones. Place in the freezer for 5 minutes to allow the chocolate to set up.

[3] Place a scoop of ice cream in the bottom of each cone, gently pressing it down in the cone.

[4] Microwave the peanut butter for 10 to 15 seconds or until pourable. Mix the pretzels and peanuts on a small plate. Drizzle about a teaspoon of the peanut butter and caramel over the ice cream. Sprinkle about a teaspoon of the pretzel twists and peanuts over the top. Place the second scoop of ice cream on top, using the scooper to create a nice round top. Roll each top into the peanuts and pretzels. Drizzle with the rest of the peanut butter and caramel. Place back in the freezer for 5 minutes.

[5] If your chocolate has hardened, microwave for 30 seconds and stir until smooth. Grab a filled ice cream cone and dip the top in the hard shell. Freeze until ready to serve. Store leftovers in the freezer.

Establish Your Go-to Dessert

Everyone needs a go-to dessert. This is the dessert you can whip up at any moment that you like to make, and that people like to eat. While I enjoy trying new recipes, having one or two recipes you consistently rely on is a game changer. The more you make the recipe, the faster you get and the easier it is to make it last minute.

Picking a Recipe

Pick a dessert you and your family enjoy and won't quickly get tired of. Sometimes, we feel pressure to make something different when we have company or go to a potluck, but if it's good, you don't need to change it up.

Another option is to pick a recipe that uses freezer or pantry ingredients but no highly perishable ones, like fresh berries, that will have you running to the grocery store at the last minute.

Here are a few of my recommendations...

1. Better Than "Better Than ANYTHING Cake" (page 197)
2. Speedy Chocolate Cake (page 132)
3. Blueberry Swirl Cheesecake (page 94)
4. Strawberry Coconut Cake (page 41)
5. Shortcut Chocolate Whoopie Pies (page 155)
6. Scotcheroo Bundt (page 121)
7. Peanut Butter Bars (page 91)

Prepare

Keep the necessary ingredients on hand to always be ready to whip up a batch. For example, if you choose to make the Shortcut Chocolate Whoopie Pies, besides basic baking ingredients, you would also keep a few chocolate cake mixes, chocolate pudding mixes, and marshmallow cream on hand. Anytime you use these ingredients, you can pick up replacements at the grocery store so you're never without them.

Make It

Next time someone invites you over to their house, instead of asking, "Is there anything I can bring?" say something like, "I can bring a blueberry cheesecake, if that sounds okay?" They announce in church that there is a potluck next Sunday. You automatically know what you're bringing. You don't have to deliberate over what to bring or run to the grocery store at the last minute—you already have it on hand.

After a while, you will start to memorize the recipe (or at least know it really well). You'll know its timing and cadence, and the baking process will flow quickly. You may feel like you've mastered your go-to recipe and be ready to add a second option to your "go-to repertoire."

Raise a Glass (or a Mug)

When my sister Tricia and I were in high school we googled funny toasts and started working to memorize them—why? I do not know. Then, one New Year's Eve, we broke them out and delivered one after the other to our family. My mom was not impressed, but my dad was laughing at most of them. There was the classic, "There are good ships and there are wood ships; there are ships that sail the sea. But the best ships are friendships, and may they always be." To honor my mom, I won't share the toast that made her lose her mind a little. But really these memorized toasts are so impersonal, and I would instead recommend a short personal toast to celebrate someone.

I should add that I don't drink and that you don't need alcohol to raise a toast. It can be whatever you have in your hand: a glass of water, a mug of coffee, or, if I'm feeling fancy, some sparkling apple cider. A toast is a great way to recognize the moment and celebrate what's important in a simple way. It takes just 30 seconds to a minute to do.

Here's a very brief formula to give a meaningful toast:

Start by opening it up by recognizing who you are honoring.

> ***I'd like to raise a toast to (guest[s] of honor).***

Share a compliment or short story about the guest. For example...

> ***Seth has been putting so much effort into his classes this quarter. He has been working diligently on his homework each night, asking questions when he doesn't understand, and studying hard for his tests. I am so proud of Seth for making the honor roll this quarter.***

Then wrap it up!

> ***So raise your glasses to (guest of honor). Cheers!***

Time for everyone to clink their glasses together!

I think we've all had to sit through a maid of honor/best man speech that seemed to never end, but these toasts are not that. They are informal snippets to make the guest of honor feel special. In our house, they can tend to the goofier side of things, and that's okay. They still do the job.

CHAPTER 7

Getting Out and Living Life

[PORTABLE TREATS]

A typical rhythm for my family on a July morning is waking up at 5 a.m., pulling out of the yard with a full trailer, and heading to one of the summer pastures. Everyone except the driver usually nods off during this time, and when we get to the pasture, we slowly wander back to the trailer door and start unloading. Then we take off—some on horseback, some on four-wheelers—and round up the cattle and trail them into the corrals. At this point, the sun is completely up, and everyone is feeling energized, breathing the cool, clean air. We sort the pairs up—cows from the calves—and then it's time for the highly anticipated break.

Someone drags the water cooler to the edge of the pickup tailgate, while someone else digs the coffee thermos out of the cab along with a few treats. It might be a cookie or a whoopie pie, but always something you can hold in your hand that's not too messy. It usually gets quiet for a little bit as everyone eats, and before we're ready for the break to be over my dad is setting up the supplies and it's time to get going again.

Life is so much better outside! Whether it's working, playing at the lake, hiking, battling it out in an intense game of pickleball, going for a run, or playing soccer, life doesn't stand still. God created a beautiful thing when He created this world, and we get to enjoy it when we head outside. If you're going to take your celebrations outside, you need a treat that can go the distance with you. This chapter features just that: sweet treats that are packable, portable, and ready for adventure!

Lemon Blueberry Cornbread Loaf

This recipe takes the typical lemon blueberry loaf and gives it some "oomph." The cornmeal adds a level of heartiness and sturdiness—perfect to pack for a day of work. I like to cut the cooled bread into thick slices, put the cut slices back together in a loaf, and wrap it in plastic wrap. This way, when it's break time, you can peel the plastic wrap back and dig in. On the go, I'll eat it as is, but if I'm at home, I like to slather butter on my slice. Because of the coarseness of the cornmeal, the blueberries will sink a bit. Coating them in flour helps, but just know they will end up sinking a bit anyway.

ACTIVE TIME: 15 minutes | **TOTAL TIME:** 1 hour 5 minutes | **YIELD:** 1 loaf

INGREDIENTS

- ¾ cup all-purpose flour
- ¾ cup yellow cornmeal
- ⅔ cup sugar
- Zest of one lemon
- 1½ teaspoons baking powder
- ½ teaspoon salt
- 6 tablespoons salted butter, softened
- ⅔ cup buttermilk
- 2 large eggs
- 1 teaspoon lemon extract
- 1½ cups fresh or frozen blueberries
- Extra tablespoon of flour

DIRECTIONS

[1] Preheat the oven to 350 degrees.

[2] Mix the flour, cornmeal, sugar, lemon zest, baking powder, and salt in a stand mixer fitted with a paddle attachment. Cut the butter into 4 chunks and add; mix until the mixture looks like wet sand.

[3] In a separate container, whisk buttermilk, eggs, and lemon extract. Pour the liquids into the flour mixture and mix until combined.

[4] Toss the blueberries in the tablespoon of flour. Dump flour-coated blueberries into the batter and stir gently using a rubber spatula.

[5] Pour the batter into a parchment-lined and greased 4½ × 8½-inch loaf pan. Bake for 30 to 40 minutes. Allow to cool. Cut into 1-inch-thick slices. Serve. Store leftovers in an airtight container.

Cardamom Fig Bar

Figs are not something I typically see in my local grocery store, but I do often see fig preserves. Fig preserves have almost a caramelly texture and flavor and pair wonderfully with the spicy, floral notes of cardamom. The homey oat crumble bar is the perfect vehicle for this flavor combo.

ACTIVE TIME: 20 minutes | **TOTAL TIME:** 1 hour 10 minutes | **YIELD:** 16 squares (2 × 2 inches)

INGREDIENTS

- ½ cup salted butter, softened
- 1 cup dark brown sugar
- 1 large egg
- 1 teaspoon vanilla extract
- 1½ cups quick oats
- 1¼ cups all-purpose flour
- ⅔ cup finely chopped walnuts
- ½ teaspoon ground cardamom
- ¼ teaspoon cinnamon
- ¼ teaspoon baking soda
- ¾ cup fig preserves

DIRECTIONS

[1] Preheat the oven to 350 degrees.

[2] Beat butter and brown sugar in a medium bowl until smooth. Add the egg and vanilla and mix until incorporated. Add oats, flour, walnuts, cardamom, cinnamon, and baking soda. Stir until combined.

[3] Spread ⅔ of the mixture into the bottom of a parchment-lined 8-inch square pan. Spread the preserves over the top. Sprinkle with the remaining dough.

[4] Bake for 25 to 30 minutes or until golden brown. Allow to cool. Slice into squares and serve. Store leftovers in an airtight container.

Shortcut Chocolate Whoopie Pies

I've heard people say the best way to eat a cupcake on the go is to split it in half horizontally, flip the frosted top over, and press it back together—kind of like a frosting sandwich. Why go to all that work when the perfect portable "cupcake" already exists? The whoopie pie. The cake bakes up with a slightly crispy edge, and the thin layers create the ideal cake-to-filling ratio with the marshmallow frosting. I often make my whoopie pies with whipped cream inside, but to keep these more "on-the-go friendly," I opted for a sturdy marshmallow buttercream.

ACTIVE TIME: 25 minutes | **TOTAL TIME:** 50 minutes | **YIELD:** 12 whoopie pies

INGREDIENTS

- ¾ cup water
- ½ cup canola oil
- 3 large eggs
- 1 (13.25 oz) pkg. chocolate cake mix
- 1 (3.4 oz.) pkg. instant chocolate pudding mix
- ½ cup salted butter, softened
- 1 cup powdered sugar
- 1 (7 oz.) pkg. marshmallow creme
- 1 teaspoon vanilla extract
- ¼ teaspoon salt

DIRECTIONS

[1] Preheat the oven to 350 degrees.

[2] Whisk water, oil, and eggs in a medium-size mixing bowl until combined.

[3] Add the cake mix and the pudding mix and whisk until smooth.

[4] Scoop batter (1½ tablespoon scoop) about 2 inches apart onto two greased baking sheets.

[5] Bake for 10 to 12 minutes, switching the baking sheets halfway through. They should spring back when gently pressed. Cool completely. Use a metal spatula to remove each cake from the pan. Match cakes into pairs—they should all be similarly sized, but try to find very close size matches for the best result.

[6] Cream the butter and powdered sugar in a stand mixer fitted with a paddle attachment until smooth. Add the marshmallow creme, vanilla, and salt. Beat until combined. Scoop (1½ tablespoon scoop) filling on the bottom of one cake and press its match on top until the filling comes to the edge. Serve. Store leftovers in an airtight container.

Almond Croissant Blondies

Almond croissants have become one of my favorite bakery treats. They're not something I ever had growing up, but I remember trying them in college and later making them at home. They're not that difficult to make, but the issue is that you have to have day-old croissants on hand, and living in the middle of nowhere makes that a little more complicated. And that's why I'm such a big fan of these almond croissant blondies. They have all the same great flavors of an almond croissant using basic pantry ingredients.

ACTIVE TIME: 20 minutes | **TOTAL TIME:** 1 hour 10 minutes | **YIELD:** 9 squares (3 × 3 inches)

INGREDIENTS

Blondie Base:

- ½ cup salted butter, melted
- 1 cup dark brown sugar
- 1 large egg
- ½ teaspoon almond extract
- 1 teaspoon vanilla extract
- 1 cup all-purpose flour
- ½ teaspoon baking powder
- ⅛ teaspoon baking soda
- Pinch of salt

Almond Filling:

- 4 tablespoons salted butter, softened
- ½ cup almond flour
- ½ cup powdered sugar
- 1½ teaspoons cornstarch
- 1 large egg
- 1½ teaspoons almond extract

Topping:

- ½ cup sliced almonds
- Powdered sugar for sifting

DIRECTIONS

[1] Preheat the oven to 350 degrees.

[2] *Prepare the blondie base.* In a medium-size mixing bowl, whisk melted butter and brown sugar. Add the egg, almond extract, and vanilla and whisk until combined.

[3] Add the flour, baking powder, soda, and salt. Use a spatula to stir until combined. Spread into a parchment-lined and sprayed 8-inch square pan.

[4] *Next, add the almond filling.* In a medium-size mixing bowl, stir the butter and almond flour until smooth. Add the powdered sugar, cornstarch, egg, and almond extract until combined. Drop teaspoons of the almond filling over the batter and swirl into the batter using a butter knife.

[5] *Now, let's put it all together.* Sprinkle with the sliced almonds and bake for 25 to 30 minutes or until the center is set. Allow to cool. Sift powdered sugar over the top. Slice into squares and serve. Store leftovers in airtight container.

Granola Blondies

Granola is a classic hiking treat, but it's not very handy to eat on the go—enter the granola blondie. This blondie is packed with oats, coconut, white chocolate chips, dried cranberries, pumpkin seeds, and pecans. Just like regular granola, where ingredients can be easily swapped for something similar, these blondies are also flexible. Swap dark chocolate chunks for white chips, sunflower seeds for pumpkin, walnuts for pecans, raisins for dried cranberries, and the list goes on! Wrap these bars in plastic wrap, throw them in your hiking bag, and whip them out when you're ready for a break.

ACTIVE TIME: 20 minutes | **TOTAL TIME:** 1 hour 10 minutes | **YIELD:** 9 bars (3 × 3-inch squares)

INGREDIENTS

- ½ cup salted butter, melted
- 1 cup dark brown sugar
- 1 large egg
- 1 teaspoon vanilla extract
- 1 cup all-purpose flour
- ½ cup quick oats
- ½ teaspoon baking powder
- ⅛ teaspoon baking soda

Mix-ins:

- ⅓ cup unsweetened shredded coconut
- ⅓ cup white chocolate chips
- ⅓ cup dried cranberries
- ⅓ cup roasted and salted pepitas
- ⅓ cup chopped raw pecans

DIRECTIONS

[1] Preheat the oven to 350 degrees.

[2] Mix butter, brown sugar, egg, and vanilla in a medium-size mixing bowl until smooth. Add flour, oats, baking powder, and baking soda, and mix until combined.

[3] Reserve about a tablespoon of each of the mix-ins.

[4] Add coconut, white chips, cranberries, pepitas, and pecans. Stir until combined. Dump the batter into a greased and parchment-lined 8-inch square pan. Press the batter into an even layer using your hands to get it into the edges and corners. Sprinkle the reserved mix-ins on top and press into the batter. Bake for 20 to 25 minutes or until golden. Allow to cool. Cut into nine squares. Serve. Store leftovers in an airtight container.

Ritz Crispy S'mores Bars

This one is for my mom. She loves camping, and her favorite treat at night is a s'more using Ritz crackers instead of graham crackers and a Reese's cup instead of the traditional chocolate bar. They are salty and rich with tons of gooey marshmallows. If you are camping, throw one of these bars on your roasting stick for a one-and-done s'more that won't have you juggling to piece together all of the different components.

ACTIVE TIME: 20 minutes | **TOTAL TIME:** 55 minutes | **YIELD:** 12 bars (2 × 3 inches)

INGREDIENTS

- ½ cup salted butter
- 1 (10 oz. pkg.) mini marshmallows (6 cups)
- 2 cups roughly crushed Ritz crackers (about 60 crackers)
- 2 cups crisp rice cereal
- 9 full-size peanut butter cups, frozen

DIRECTIONS

[1] Melt butter in a large microwave-safe dish for 30 seconds. Add marshmallows and cook for another 2 minutes. Stir until the mixture is smooth. Add the crackers and cereal and stir until coated. Allow the mixture to cool for 15 minutes.

[2] Chop the frozen peanut butter cups into small chunks. Gently stir the peanut butter cups into the cereal/cracker mixture and press into a greased and parchment-lined 9-inch square pan. Refrigerate until firm. Cut into rectangles. Serve. If desired, roast using a roasting stick over a campfire until the marshmallow caramelizes and the chocolate is melted. Store leftovers in an airtight container.

Biscoff Coffee Banana Pudding

I always look forward to enjoying Biscoff cookies and coffee when I'm flying. And while I'm a big fan of that Biscoff and coffee combo, I'm an even bigger fan of this new blend of Biscoff, coffee, butterscotch, and banana. It sounds like a lot going on, but these flavors harmonize so well together you'll wonder where this recipe has been all your life. Pack these jars in a cooler and enjoy lakeside or wherever you end up for the day. Don't forget to pack spoons!

ACTIVE TIME: 30 minutes | **TOTAL TIME:** 2 hours | **YIELD:** 12 servings (8 oz. jars)

INGREDIENTS

- Microwave Butterscotch (page 211)
- 1 (14 oz.) can sweetened condensed milk
- 1½ cups water
- 1 (3.4 oz.) pkg. instant vanilla pudding mix
- 1 tablespoon instant coffee
- 1 teaspoon vanilla extract
- 3 cups heavy whipping cream
- 1 (8.8 oz.) pkg. Biscoff cookies
- 4 ripe but firm bananas, sliced

DIRECTIONS

[1] Prepare Microwave Butterscotch according to recipe directions. Refrigerate until chilled.

[2] Whisk sweetened condensed milk and water in a medium-size bowl. Add the pudding mix, instant coffee, and vanilla. Whisk until smooth. Refrigerate until set, about an hour.

[3] Whip the heavy cream until it has medium peaks. Gently stir the whipped cream into the pudding mixture.

[4] Layer cookies into 12 (8 oz.) jars (break cookies if needed to fit them into your jars), then sliced bananas, butterscotch, and finally the creamy coffee/pudding mixture. Chill for 4 to 6 hours to allow the cookies to soften. Serve. Store leftovers in the fridge.

NOTE: If you're staying put and don't need a portable dessert, layer up these components into a trifle bowl. Not only does it simplify the layering process, it results in a stunning statuesque dessert.

Browned Butter Malted Chunk Cookies

Chocolate chip cookies are the OG portable treat, and this recipe gives the classic version a run for its money. The recipe starts with browned butter, adding a nutty nuance to the cookies. If you've ever had an ice cream malt, the malted barley flavor is unlike anything else and adds another layer of interest to this cookie. These cookies are packed with white chocolate and bittersweet chocolate chunks and topped with flaky sea salt. They are anything but typical.

ACTIVE TIME: 25 minutes | **TOTAL TIME:** 1 hour 20 minutes | **YIELD:** 16 cookies

INGREDIENTS

- ½ cup salted butter
- ½ cup sugar
- ½ cup dark brown sugar
- 1 large egg
- 1 teaspoon vanilla extract
- 1 cup all-purpose flour
- ⅓ cup malted milk powder (original flavor)
- ½ teaspoon baking soda
- ½ teaspoon baking powder
- ¼ teaspoon salt
- 4 oz. bittersweet chocolate, roughly chopped
- 2 oz. white chocolate, roughly chopped
- Flaky sea salt (optional)

DIRECTIONS

[1] Heat butter in a small saucepan over medium heat, swirling occasionally, until it turns golden and has a nutty aroma. Pour the browned butter into a medium-sized mixing bowl or stand mixer bowl and allow to cool for 15 minutes.

[2] Add sugar and brown sugar and stir until smooth. Add the egg and vanilla and combine.

[3] Add flour, malted milk powder, baking soda, baking powder, and salt. Mix until combined. Add the chopped chocolate and stir until it is distributed throughout the dough.

[4] Transfer the dough to a cutting board and pat into a rectangle that is about 6 × 6 inches. The size doesn't need to be exact; it's just to help portion the cookies. Refrigerate for 30 minutes.

[5] Preheat the oven to 350 degrees. Cut the square into 16 portions by first cutting it into fourths with a bench scraper and then cutting each fourth into four equal pieces. You don't need to roll them into balls, but do pinch in the corners to create a disk so you don't get a square cookie. Space them 2 to 3 inches apart on a parchment-lined baking sheet.

[6] Bake for 8 to 12 minutes or until golden brown. Remove the pan from the oven and bang the bottom of the pan on a heatproof surface. This deflates the cookie and creates the ripples on the edges. Continue to bake in batches until all of the dough has been used. Sprinkle flaky sea salt over the cookies, if desired. Allow to cool slightly and serve. Store in an airtight container.

Cinnamon Oatmeal Cream Pies

These oatmeal cream pies start by grinding oats into a powder and then mixing up the batter, producing chewy, cakey cookies that taste even better filled with cinnamon buttercream. I experimented with leaving the oats whole and blitzing them in the food processor and found that breaking them down produced a similar texture to the popular snack cakes. I think you're really going to like this one!

ACTIVE TIME: 25 minutes | **TOTAL TIME:** 55 minutes | **YIELD:** 10 sandwich cookies

INGREDIENTS

Cookie:

- 1½ cups quick oats
- ½ cup salted butter, softened
- 1 cup dark brown sugar
- 2 large eggs
- 2 tablespoons molasses
- 1 teaspoon vanilla extract
- ¾ cup all-purpose flour
- ½ teaspoon baking powder
- ½ teaspoon ground cinnamon
- ¼ teaspoon baking soda
- ¼ teaspoon salt

Buttercream:

- ½ cup salted butter, softened
- 1¾ cups powdered sugar
- 2 teaspoons heavy whipping cream
- ½ teaspoon ground cinnamon
- Pinch of salt

DIRECTIONS

[1] Preheat the oven to 350 degrees.

[2] *Prepare the cookie base.* Blitz the oats in a blender or food processor until it is mostly a powder with only a few oat bits remaining.

[3] Cream the butter and brown sugar in a stand mixer fitted with the paddle attachment until smooth. Add the eggs, molasses, and vanilla and mix until incorporated. Add the oat powder, flour, baking powder, cinnamon, baking soda, and salt. Stir until combined.

[4] Scoop the dough into 1½ tablespoon balls on a parchment-lined baking sheet and space them about 2 inches apart. Bake for 8 to 12 minutes or until the cookie is set and doesn't look wet in the middle. Continue to bake in batches until all of the dough has been used. Allow to cool completely.

[5] *Now, make the buttercream and put it all together.* Cream the butter and powdered sugar until smooth. Add the heavy cream, cinnamon, and salt. Mix until smooth. Place half of the cookies bottom side up. Scoop about 1 tablespoon buttercream on the cookie bottoms. Top with the other half of the cookies. Press down gently until the frosting squishes to the edges of the cookie. Store leftovers in an airtight container.

Peanut Butter Chocolate Chip Snacking Cake

If you've never heard of a "snacking cake," it's a cake that comes together quickly, isn't usually frosted, and can be picked up and eaten with your hands. In this moist, craveable cake, peanut butter and brown sugar batter gets studded with mini chocolate chips.

ACTIVE TIME: 20 minutes | **TOTAL TIME:** 1 hour 20 minutes | **YIELD:** 9 servings

INGREDIENTS

- 1 cup dark brown sugar
- ½ cup creamy peanut butter
- ¼ cup whole milk
- ¼ cup sour cream
- ⅓ cup water
- ¼ cup canola oil
- 1 large egg
- 1 teaspoon vanilla extract
- 1 cup all-purpose flour
- 2 tablespoons cornstarch
- ¾ teaspoon baking powder
- ¾ teaspoon baking soda
- ¾ teaspoon salt
- 1¼ cup mini chocolate chips, divided

DIRECTIONS

[1] Preheat the oven to 350 degrees.

[2] Mix brown sugar, peanut butter, milk, sour cream, water, oil, egg, and vanilla in a stand mixer fitted with the paddle attachment until smooth.

[3] Add flour, cornstarch, baking powder, baking soda, and salt. Mix until just combined. Mix 1 cup of chocolate chips into the batter.

[4] Pour the batter into a greased and parchment-lined 9-inch square pan. Sprinkle the remaining chocolate chips over the top. Bake for 25 to 28 minutes or until a toothpick inserted comes out with moist crumbs. Cool completely. Cut into squares and serve. Store leftovers in an airtight container.

Tips to Package and Transport Desserts

Cut Ahead of Time

While you're still at home, cut your bars, loaf, or cake so they are ready to grab and go. If you think some people may prefer a smaller portion, cut a few into half slices so you don't have to mess around trying to break your treats in half outside.

Wrap It Up

If you cut a loaf or cake ahead of time, you can risk it drying out. To prevent this, cut it into slices and then put it "back together" so that the cut sides touch each other. Finally, wrap the entire cake in plastic wrap to keep the moisture in. You can also individually wrap bars, blondies, whoopie pies, and so on, to keep them moist and easier to pass around. But blondies and bars are sturdy and don't need to be wrapped if they are eaten in the first few days.

Box It Up

Put any of your wrapped treats into a box—whether cardboard, glass, or a plastic storage container. This will prevent them from getting smashed when you're loading up.

Cooler

When transporting parfaits, they need to be kept in a cooler with ice or ice packs. If you are using sturdy jars or containers, you can put them pretty much anywhere in your cooler. If you are headed out on a sweltering and sunny day, any portable treat with chocolate will benefit from being placed at the very top of your cooler in a hard-sided storage container to prevent it from getting smashed.

CHAPTER 8

Slow Mornings Together

[BREAKFAST SWEETS]

Even though I am not a morning person, mornings are one of my favorite times. I specifically love slow mornings. The type of mornings you're not rushing off to work or frantically packing lunches, but instead the mornings where you get the luxury of slowing down.

When my sisters and I went to boarding school in high school, four hours away from home, each week was filled with chaos—school, sports, early morning gratis, late-night chats, evening study hall—needless to say, it was packed. I always say high school was the busiest time of my life. But every Friday night we would drive home and fall into our beds happy to be home and so exhausted. Saturday morning was the sweetest time, as we would wake up slowly and sit around the table and chat and eat our breakfast at a leisurely pace.

I also think my breakfast memories are some of my favorites. Mornings are special because they are a time when we are authentic, not trying to impress anyone. We are often at our most vulnerable with no makeup, hair sticking up, or sleepy eyes. These breakfast sweets recipes can be made in a reasonable amount of time or are able to be made the day before; otherwise, they're less like morning treats and more like dessert for lunch.

Apple Strudel

When I was student teaching in Omaha, my sister Ann and our friend Amanda and I would occasionally go to a restaurant nearby—Wheatfields. We would get there right when it opened—6:30 a.m.—and have the place to ourselves. I would always order the apple strudel. It was fresh from the oven, filled with tender spicy apples and flaky, crispy pastry, and they would serve it with a bowl of rich, sweet cream. This recipe gets very close to the original and is made easier with the use of puff pastry.

ACTIVE TIME: 35 minutes | **TOTAL TIME:** 55 minutes | **YIELD:** 2 braids, 10–15 servings

INGREDIENTS

- 2 medium Granny Smith apples
- ½ cup dark brown sugar
- ⅓ cup raisins
- 1 teaspoon ground cinnamon
- ¼ teaspoon ground nutmeg
- 1 tablespoon all-purpose flour
- 1 (17.3 oz.) pkg. frozen puff pastry, thawed
- 1 large egg
- 2 tablespoons raw sugar

Cream:

- 2 oz. cream cheese, softened
- ⅓ cup powdered sugar
- 1 cup heavy whipping cream
- ½ teaspoon vanilla extract

DIRECTIONS

[1] Preheat the oven to 400 degrees.

[2] Peel, core, and thinly slice the apples. Toss the apples, brown sugar, raisins, cinnamon, nutmeg, and flour until the apples are coated.

[3] Unfold the puff pastry sheets onto parchment paper and use a rolling pin to smooth out the creases. Split the apple filling between the two pastries, placing it in the middle third of the dough; it should be about 3 inches wide. Cut 1-inch-wide strips on a diagonal on both the left and right sides of the filling. Fold the strips over the filling, alternating left and right until all of the strips have been folded in. Tuck the ends of the braid under.

[4] Whisk the egg and brush the top of the pastry with the egg wash. Sprinkle each braid with a tablespoon of raw sugar. Bake for 15 to 18 minutes or until golden. Allow to cool slightly. Cut into pieces that are 1 to 2 inches wide.

[5] Cream the cream cheese and powdered sugar using a rubber spatula in a liquid measuring cup until smooth. Add the heavy cream and vanilla and whip using an immersion blender until soft peaks form. Transfer the cream to a bowl and serve it with the strudel. People can dip their strudel into the cream or spoon generous dollops on each piece. This is best enjoyed immediately, but refrigerate any leftovers in an airtight container.

Ultimate Almond Poppy Seed Muffins

On a vacation to Cannon Beach, Oregon, my family picked up some delicious pastries one morning, including an odd-looking "upside-down" muffin. After cutting all of the pastries into quarters, giving everyone the chance to try several options, this almond poppy muffin emerged as a favorite. It's moist and features the flavor of almond extract paired with the poppy seeds' texture—it's a winner. The upside-down look seems a bit random at first, but it provides more surface area for the tasty almondy glaze to cover. These muffins can't be in muffin liners since the glaze is over the bottom, but there's nothing worse than having your muffins get stuck in the pan. To prevent the muffins from sticking, I heat the muffin pan in the oven and grease it before adding the batter—just like if you were cooking eggs, you get the pan nice and hot so they don't stick.

ACTIVE TIME: 25 minutes | **TOTAL TIME:** 50 minutes | **YIELD:** 1 dozen muffins

INGREDIENTS

Muffins:

- 6 tablespoons salted butter, melted
- ¼ cup canola oil
- 1 cup sugar
- 1 large egg
- 1 large egg yolk
- ½ cup sour cream
- ¼ cup whole milk
- 1 teaspoon almond extract
- 1⅓ cups all-purpose flour
- 3 tablespoons cornstarch
- 2 tablespoons poppy seeds
- ¾ teaspoon baking powder
- ¼ teaspoon baking soda
- ¼ teaspoon salt

Glaze:

- 1 cup powdered sugar
- 6 tablespoons heavy whipping cream
- ¾ teaspoon almond extract
- ½ teaspoon vanilla extract

DIRECTIONS

[1] Preheat the oven to 350 degrees. Place a 12-cup muffin tin in the cold oven.

[2] *Make your muffin batter.* Whisk melted butter, oil, and sugar in a medium-size mixing bowl until smooth. Add egg, egg yolk, sour cream, milk, and almond extract and whisk until combined. Add flour, cornstarch, poppy seeds, baking powder, baking soda, and salt with a rubber spatula until combined.

[3] Once your oven is preheated, remove the muffin tin. Very generously spray each well with nonstick cooking spray. Let sit for 30 seconds (this gives the oil a chance to heat up). Scoop about ⅓ cup of batter into each well. Be careful—the pan is hot!

[4] Bake for 15 to 18 minutes. Remove muffins from the oven. While they are still hot, quickly run a butter knife around the edge of each muffin. Use oven mitts to invert the muffin tin onto a parchment-lined sheet pan and give the muffin pan a bang on the tray to help the muffins come out. Flip over any muffins that are right side up.

[5] *Now, make the glaze.* Whisk powdered sugar, heavy cream, almond extract, and vanilla in a small bowl until smooth. Dip each muffin bottom into the glaze using your hands. (Things might get messy!) Serve. Store leftovers in an airtight container.

Chocolate Orange Bostock

Bostock is the cousin of the French pastry—the almond croissant. It uses day-old bread in place of the croissant while still using frangipane. Think of it like an open-face almond croissant, but in this variation, I added orange and bittersweet chocolate to mix it up. This morning treat balances textures and flavors nicely with the crispy bread, chewy frangipane, bright orange flavor, subtle almond flavor, and rich chocolate chunks.

ACTIVE TIME: 20 minutes | **TOTAL TIME:** 50 minutes | **YIELD:** 8 servings

INGREDIENTS

- 1 medium orange
- ¼ cup sugar
- 6 slices brioche bread

Frangipane:

- ¼ cup salted butter, softened
- ⅔ cup almond flour
- ½ cup powdered sugar
- 1½ teaspoons cornstarch
- 1 large egg
- ½ teaspoon almond extract
- 1 (4 oz.) bittersweet chocolate bar, chopped
- Powdered sugar for sifting

DIRECTIONS

[1] Preheat the oven to 375 degrees.

[2] Zest the orange into a medium-size mixing bowl; set aside. Juice the orange, measuring ¼ cup juice.

[3] Heat the orange juice and sugar in the microwave for 45 seconds. Stir until the sugar dissolves. Brush each side of the bread with the syrup using a pastry brush and place them on a parchment-lined baking sheet.

[4] Into the bowl with the orange zest, add the butter, almond flour, powdered sugar, and cornstarch; cream until smooth. Add the egg and almond extract. Mix until combined. Spread a generous 2 tablespoons of the frangipane on each piece of bread using a butter knife.

[5] Arrange the chopped chocolate over the top. Bake for 12 to 15 minutes or until lightly browned. Use a metal spatula to check the bottoms to ensure they do not get too dark. Allow them to cool for 10 minutes. Sift powdered sugar over the top. Serve. Store leftovers in an airtight container.

Smothered Blueberry Lemon Scones

Scones often get accused of being dry; these scones will never be guilty of that. This recipe starts off with my popular scone recipe, which is moist in its own right, but that is only the beginning. The scones then get covered in generous portions of whipped cream and lemon curd. In fact, these scones are so smothered that you can barely see the scones under all of the tasty toppings. To keep your morning more relaxing, prep the scone dough disk and lemon curd the day before and then cut and bake the scones the next morning.

ACTIVE TIME: 35 minutes | **TOTAL TIME:** 3 hours 25 minutes | **YIELD:** 8 servings

INGREDIENTS

- 1 cup Lemon Curd (page 212)

Scones:

- 2 cups all-purpose flour
- ½ cup sugar
- 1 tablespoon baking powder
- ½ teaspoon salt
- ¾ cup very cold salted butter
- ⅓ cup + 1 tablespoon whole milk
- 1 large egg
- 1 cup fresh blueberries
- 1 tablespoon heavy whipping cream

Cream:

- 1 cup heavy whipping cream
- ⅓ cup powdered sugar
- ½ teaspoon vanilla extract

DIRECTIONS

[1] Prepare the Lemon Curd according to recipe directions. Refrigerate until chilled.

[2] Whisk the flour, sugar, baking powder, and salt in a medium-size mixing bowl.

[3] Grate the butter into the dry mixture. Use your hands to toss and coat the butter in the flour and break it into smaller pieces.

[4] Whisk the milk and egg in a small bowl. Add it to the flour mixture and stir using a spatula until the dough gets shaggy. Add the blueberries. Stir gently until combined.

[5] Dump the dough onto a large piece of plastic wrap and loosely wrap it. Press the dough into a disk that is ¾ inches thick and about 8 inches across. Use your hands to shape the dough through the plastic wrap. Refrigerate for 30 minutes.

[6] Preheat the oven to 400 degrees. Unwrap the disk and use a bench scraper or a chef's knife to cut it into eight wedges. Space the wedges on a 13 × 18-inch parchment-lined baking sheet.

[7] Using a pastry brush, brush heavy cream over each scone. Bake for 16 to 20 minutes or until golden. Cool completely.

[8] Whip the cup of heavy cream with the powdered sugar and vanilla in a stand mixer fitted with the whisk attachment until soft peaks form. To serve, top scones with generous dollops of the whipped cream and the lemon curd. Serve. Store leftover cream and curd in the fridge.

Blueberry Crumble Coffee Cake

This recipe has been a favorite for years with good reason—juicy blueberries, tender cake, salty crumble, and vanilla glaze. I love anytime I can make a recipe more efficient. I created this recipe when trying to develop a blueberry muffin recipe, but I didn't want to take all the time to scoop each muffin out and sprinkle on the topping. I also adjusted the ratios of cake and crumble, resulting in a crumble-forward cake that you wouldn't be able to achieve in a muffin tin, as this much crumble would start falling off your typical muffin. A drizzle of vanilla glaze brings it all together.

ACTIVE TIME: 30 minutes | **TOTAL TIME:** 1 hour 15 minutes | **YIELD:** 24 servings (3 × 3- inch squares)

INGREDIENTS

Batter:

- 6 tablespoons salted butter, softened
- ⅔ cup sugar
- 2 large eggs
- 1 teaspoon vanilla extract
- 1 cup all-purpose flour
- ¾ teaspoon baking soda
- ¾ teaspoon baking powder
- Pinch of salt
- ⅓ cup sour cream
- 2 tablespoons whole milk
- 1½ cups fresh blueberries, or thawed if frozen

Crumble:

- ½ cup salted butter, melted
- ⅓ cup dark brown sugar
- ⅓ cup white sugar
- 1 cup + 2 tablespoons all-purpose flour
- 2 tablespoons cornstarch
- 1 teaspoon ground cinnamon
- Pinch of salt

Glaze:

- 1 cup powdered sugar
- ¼ cup heavy whipping cream
- ½ teaspoon vanilla extract

DIRECTIONS

[1] Preheat the oven to 350 degrees.

[2] *Make the batter.* In a stand mixer fitted with the paddle attachment, beat butter and sugar on medium speed until smooth and fluffy. Add the eggs and vanilla and beat until incorporated.

[3] Add flour, baking soda, baking powder, and salt, and stir on low until just combined.

[4] Add the sour cream and milk and stir until smooth.

[5] Using an offset spatula, spread the batter onto a greased and parchment-lined 9 × 13-inch pan. Sprinkle the blueberries over the top.

[6] *Now, prepare the crumble.* Mix the melted butter, brown sugar, and white sugar in a medium-sized mixing bowl until smooth. Add flour, cornstarch, cinnamon, and salt, and stir until combined. Use your fingers to break the crumble up and sprinkle over the blueberries.

[7] Bake for 20-25 minutes or until golden brown and set in the middle. Allow it to cool slightly.

[8] *Top it off with the glaze.* Whisk the powdered sugar, heavy cream, and vanilla until smooth. Transfer the glaze to a piping bag or use your whisk to drizzle the glaze evenly over the cake. Serve. Store leftovers in an airtight container.

Shortcut Coconut Malasadas

These Shortcut Coconut Malasadas are inspired by the classic Portuguese donuts you might see in Hawaii (and in one of my favorite TV shows: Hawaii Five-0*). These "faux-nuts" cut down on the prep time of typical malasadas by using dinner rolls. My favorite part is that you don't even need to shape the rolls; just let them thaw and rise and then fry them up. Coconut Cream is reminiscent of the classic coconut pudding or haupia that is found in some malasada variations.*

ACTIVE TIME: 1 hour | **TOTAL TIME:** 9 hours 15 minutes | **YIELD:** 2 dozen

INGREDIENTS

- Coconut Cream (page 213)
- 24 frozen dinner roll dough balls
- ½ cup sugar
- Oil for frying

DIRECTIONS

[1] Prepare the Coconut Cream according to the recipe directions.

[2] Space frozen dinner rolls an inch apart on a generously greased baking sheet. Cover loosely with plastic wrap. Refrigerate to thaw overnight or for 8 to 12 hours.

[3] Remove the rolls from the fridge and allow to rise at room temperature for one hour or until they are doubled in size.

[4] Pour oil 2 to 3 inches deep in a large, heavy-bottom pot. I like to use my Dutch oven. Heat over medium heat until the oil reaches 360 degrees. Prep your frying station with a sheet tray covered with layers of paper towels, and pour sugar into a shallow bowl.

[5] Add the donuts carefully to the hot oil, frying them in small batches of 3 to 4 (depending on the size of your pot). Cook the donuts for about 1 to 2 minutes on each side. Keep an eye on the donuts and flip them with a slotted metal spatula when they are a deep golden brown. Once both sides are golden brown, remove them from the oil and place them on the paper towel–lined tray. Once the donuts are just cool enough to handle, roll them in sugar. Continue frying and rolling until you have fried all of the donuts. Allow them to cool for 15 minutes.

[6] Transfer coconut cream to a piping bag and snip a ½-inch-size hole. Use a straw, skewer, chopstick, or whatever you have to create a hole in the side of each donut. Do not poke all of the way through; this is simply creating a cavity in the middle for the filling.

[7] Push the corner of the piping bag into the malasada and squeeze to fill each donut with coconut cream. Serve. Store leftovers in the fridge. They are best enjoyed within the first few hours.

TIP: I have a very good nose, and no matter how many windows I have open or if I have the vent running, I can still smell the "fried" smell in my house after making these donuts. If possible, I like to use a portable burner on the deck, or if you have a grill with a side burner, that will also work to keep the smell outside. Just be careful. You may attract the neighbors. You've been warned!

White Chocolate Raspberry Crepe Platter

This crepe platter is impressive, and I love the visual impact of this bright red and pink dessert. White chocolate desserts can become cloyingly sweet—not this one. The tart raspberry filling and fresh raspberries provide a lovely balance. To make things easier for yourself, prep the crepes and the raspberry filling the day before. This entire platter can be made the day before. In fact, I have assembled this platter in a storage container, thrown it in our cooler, and taken these crepes on a camping trip.

ACTIVE TIME: 1 hour 10 minutes | **TOTAL TIME:** 2 hours 30 minutes | **YIELD:** 8–12 servings

INGREDIENTS

- Crepes (page 218)
- 1 cup Two-Ingredient Raspberry Filling (page 213)

Cream:

- 2 cups heavy cream
- ⅔ cup powdered sugar
- 3 tablespoons white chocolate instant pudding mix
- 6 oz. fresh raspberries
- 1 oz. white chocolate

DIRECTIONS

[1] Prepare the Crepes, layering them between pieces of parchment paper to prevent them from sticking, and refrigerate until chilled.

[2] Prepare the Two-Ingredient Raspberry Filling according to the recipe directions. Strain the seeds out of the filling using a sieve. You may need to use a spatula to work the filling through the sieve. Refrigerate until chilled.

[3] Whip the heavy cream, powdered sugar, pudding mix, and ⅔ cup of the strained raspberry filling in a stand mixer fitted with a whisk attachment until soft peaks form.

[4] Spread about 2 tablespoons of the cream using an offset spatula only on half of each crepe. Fold in half and half again so that the crepe is in quarters. Arrange the filled crepes on a serving platter.

[5] Dollop leftover cream over the crepes. Drizzle the remaining raspberry filling over the crepes. Sprinkle raspberries over the top. Scrape a vegetable peeler across the white chocolate to create white chocolate curls as a finishing touch. Serve. Store leftovers in the refrigerator.

Double Dutch Baby

This pancake has nothing to do with jump roping but gets its name from the combination of the internet favorite Dutch baby and the Dutch Honey recipe I learned from our neighbors the Flatmoes. If you've never had Dutch honey, it has no honey but is the combination of heavy cream and brown sugar. It's a caramelly addictive syrup that's so good you may never want to go back to maple. It's the perfect balance for the simple canvas of the Dutch baby that is custardy and crispy but relatively simple in taste. Since it is breakfast, I tone down the sweetness even further with Greek yogurt, bananas, and blueberries.

ACTIVE TIME: 15 minutes | **TOTAL TIME:** 30 minutes | **YIELD:** 4–6 servings

INGREDIENTS

Dutch Baby:

- 3 large eggs
- ½ cup all-purpose flour
- ½ cup whole milk
- 1 tablespoon sugar
- Pinch of cinnamon
- Pinch of nutmeg
- 2 tablespoons butter

Dutch Honey:

- ½ cup heavy whipping cream
- ½ cup dark brown sugar

Toppings:

- ½ cup plain Greek yogurt
- 1 medium banana, peeled and sliced
- ½ cup fresh blueberries, or thawed if frozen

DIRECTIONS

[1] Preheat the oven to 425 degrees. Place a cast-iron skillet in the cold oven.

[2] Blend eggs, flour, milk, sugar, cinnamon, and nutmeg in a blender or a liquid measuring cup using an immersion blender.

[3] When the oven is preheated, remove the pan and add the butter. Use a fork to swirl the butter as it begins to melt. Place the pan back in the oven for another 30 seconds or until the butter is melted. Remove the pan again and pour the batter into the center of the pan. Bake for 13 to 15 minutes or until golden and puffy. Allow to cool for 5 minutes.

[4] While the Dutch baby is baking, whisk the heavy cream and brown sugar in a small bowl for a couple of minutes until the sugar dissolves. Microwave for 1 minute or until it is warm.

[5] Pour ¼ cup of the Dutch honey in a small bowl and mix it with the Greek yogurt until combined. Transfer the rest of the Dutch honey to a small serving bowl.

[6] Top the Dutch baby with yogurt, banana slices, and blueberries. You can serve the honey over the top or on the side so everyone can add it according to their sweetness preference.

[7] Cut it into wedges and serve. Store leftovers in the refrigerator.

Pumpkin Crumble Coffee Cake

One fall, I was looking to develop a pumpkin recipe that was simple to make and didn't have too many steps, and this Pumpkin Crumble Coffee Cake was born! I started by creating a simple pumpkin cake that was moist without being too dense. I then adjusted the crumble from my Blueberry Crumble Coffee Cake (page 178) and added pecans to drive home the fall flavors and add a nice crunch. The final touch was to whip up an effortless maple glaze and drizzle it over the top.

ACTIVE TIME: 25 minutes | **TOTAL TIME:** 1 hour 15 minutes | **YIELD:** 8 servings

INGREDIENTS

Cake:

- 1 cup all-purpose flour
- 1 teaspoon baking powder
- ½ teaspoon baking soda
- ¼ teaspoon salt
- 2 teaspoons pumpkin pie spice
- 1 cup pumpkin puree
- ½ cup canola oil
- 2 large eggs
- ¼ cup light brown sugar
- ½ cup sugar

Crumble:

- 2½ tablespoons salted butter, melted
- ¼ cup all-purpose flour
- ¼ cup light brown sugar
- ½ cup chopped pecans
- ¼ teaspoon salt

Glaze:

- ⅔ cup powdered sugar
- 2½ tablespoons heavy cream
- ¼ teaspoon maple extract

DIRECTIONS

[1] Preheat the oven to 350 degrees.

[2] In a small bowl, whisk the cup of flour with the baking powder, baking soda, salt, and pumpkin pie spice. In a separate bowl, whisk the pumpkin, oil, eggs, brown sugar, and sugar.

[3] Dump the dry ingredients into the pumpkin mixture and stir until just combined. Pour the pumpkin batter into a greased and parchment-lined 8-inch cake pan.

[4] Stir the crumble ingredients in a small bowl until combined. Use your fingers to break up the crumble and sprinkle it over the top of the batter. Bake for 30 to 35 minutes. Allow to cool.

[5] Whisk powdered sugar, heavy cream, and maple extract in a small bowl until smooth. Transfer it to a piping bag. Snip a small corner and drizzle it over the cake. Cut into wedges and serve. Store leftovers in an airtight container.

Maple Brown Butter Cinnamon Rolls

I like trying different recipes. Can you tell? But my family has let me know more than once that they would be just as happy if I only made these cinnamon rolls for the rest of their lives. These cinnamon rolls feature a very hydrated dough that produces a gooey, tender roll and is finished with a scrumptious maple brown butter glaze. To achieve a stress-free morning, you must make the dough the night before and then finish the rolls when you wake up.

ACTIVE TIME: 45 minutes | **TOTAL TIME:** 10 hours 40 minutes | **YIELD:** 9 rolls

INGREDIENTS

Dough:

- 1 cup whole milk
- 2 tablespoons salted butter, melted
- 2 tablespoons canola oil
- ¼ cup sugar
- 1¼ teaspoon dry active yeast
- 2 cups all-purpose flour, divided
- ½ teaspoon baking powder
- ½ teaspoon salt

Filling:

- ¼ cup salted butter, melted
- ⅓ cup sugar
- 2 teaspoons ground cinnamon

Glaze:

- 2 tablespoons salted butter
- 2 cups powdered sugar
- ¼ cup heavy whipping cream
- ½ teaspoon maple extract
- Pinch of salt

DIRECTIONS

[1] Heat milk, butter, oil, and sugar in a microwave-safe dish for 1½ minutes or until hot and steamy.

[2] Transfer to a mixing bowl, and allow the milk mixture to cool to about 110 degrees. This will take 10 to 15 minutes. It needs to be warm enough to activate the yeast but not so hot that it kills it. Add the yeast. Let the yeast sit on top of the milk for a few minutes before whisking it in.

[3] Add 1½ cups flour and stir until smooth. Cover with a kitchen towel or plastic wrap, and allow the dough to rise for about 45 minutes or until doubled in size.

[4] Add the remaining ½ cup of flour, baking powder, and salt. Stir until smooth. Cover and refrigerate overnight or until chilled.

[5] Roll the dough into a rectangle about 12 × 15 inches, about ¼ inch thick, on a floured surface.

[6] In a small mixing bowl, mix the filling ingredients until smooth.

[7] Spread the cinnamon filling evenly over the dough. Roll up tightly, starting at the long edge.

[8] Slice into 9 rolls about 1½ inches thick. Place rolls in a greased and parchment-lined 9-inch square pan. Preheat the oven to 375 degrees while you allow the rolls to rise for 20 to 30 minutes. Bake for 20 to 25 minutes or until golden.

[9] Once the rolls have come out of the oven, make the glaze. Heat butter in a small saucepan over medium heat, swirling occasionally, until it turns golden and has a nutty aroma. Remove from the heat. Add the powdered sugar, heavy cream, maple extract, and salt and whisk until smooth. It should be a pourable consistency. If it is still a bit thick, add cream, one tablespoon cream at a time, until it is pourable. Pour the glaze over the warm cinnamon rolls and serve. Store leftovers in an airtight container.

Coconut Croissant

It's no secret that I love almond-flavored anything, including almond croissants, but this recipe flips the script and gives the classic almond croissant a coconut spin. This twice-baked pastry takes day-old croissants, dips them in a coconut syrup, fills them with a coconut frangipane, and finishes them off with more coconut flakes. The final product is a pastry with crispy edges and a chewy center. I am not able to get croissants in my local small-town grocery store, so I like to keep my freezer stocked so I can make these whenever the urge strikes.

ACTIVE TIME: 20 minutes | **TOTAL TIME:** 50 minutes | **YIELD:** 6 croissants

INGREDIENTS

- 6 day-old croissants

Syrup:

- ⅓ cup boiling water
- ⅓ cup sugar
- 1 teaspoon coconut extract

Filling:

- ⅓ cup salted butter, softened
- ⅔ cup almond flour
- ½ cup powdered sugar
- ½ cup coconut flakes
- 2 teaspoons cornstarch
- Pinch of salt
- ½ teaspoon coconut extract
- 1 large egg

Topping:

- ⅓ cup unsweetened coconut flakes
- Powdered sugar

DIRECTIONS

[1] Preheat the oven to 400 degrees. Cut each croissant in half and set aside.

[2] Mix the boiling water, sugar, and 1 teaspoon coconut extract until the sugar is dissolved. Allow the syrup to cool.

[3] Cream the butter, almond flour, powdered sugar, ½ cup coconut, cornstarch, salt, and ½ teaspoon coconut extract until smooth. Add the egg and mix until no lumps remain.

[4] Use a pastry brush to coat all sides of each croissant half with the coconut syrup. Reserve 2 tablespoons of the filling to top the croissants. Spread about 2 tablespoons of the filling mixture on the bottom half of each croissant and replace each croissant top.

[5] Place the ⅓ cup coconut flakes on a small plate.

[6] Spread a teaspoon of the reserved filling on top of each croissant and press it into the coconut flakes.

[7] Bake for 14 to 16 minutes or until golden brown and crispy. Sift powdered sugar over the top. Best enjoyed immediately, but store leftovers in an airtight container.

"This Is Us" Morning Picture or Video

Some of my favorite memories are the slow mornings when you wake up without a blaring alarm clock and a full schedule. Everyone slowly makes their way to the kitchen in their pajamas—no makeup, whatever hairdo you rolled out of bed in, and fun, lighthearted conversation. This is some of the sweetest time a family can experience. Breakfast is not a meal we often share with people. It's the time of day when we are the most real and our true selves. So, take out your phone and capture the memory!

I have a feeling you might think I've lost my mind with this one, but I suggest that when you are all gathered around the breakfast table, you snap a photo or take a quick video. Let's first be clear—this is not a picture that you're going to post to social media, so all of the teen girls and middle-aged women can pop a chill pill. Just kidding. This picture is just for you and your family.

In twenty years or even just ten years, you'll look at this and say, "Wow! We look so young/they look so little." I also think this is especially sweet with siblings. We grow up and get married and, sadly, are rarely together for these sweet times, but having the memories in picture or video form keeps that time alive.

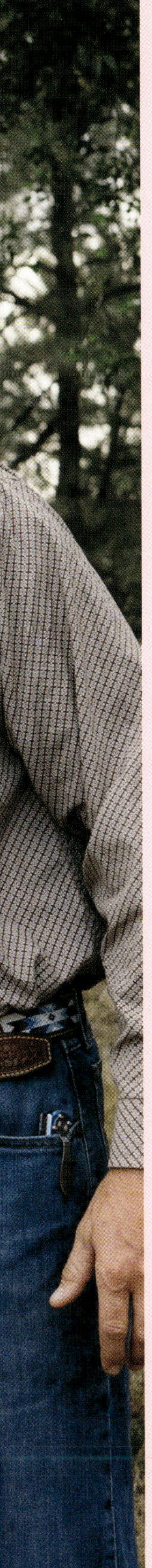

CHAPTER 9

Building Community

[SHARABLE SHEET PAN DESSERTS]

Recently my family hosted a comedy night at our ranch—not very common out on the prairie. We had round tables and chairs set up on our cement driveway/basketball court, café lights overhead, and a bonfire. Our friends Mick and Rick, twin comedians from Alabama, had everyone roaring.

Over the last few decades, we have hosted numerous parties, but these community-building events can be more than just "parties." They can also be centered around working together, like branding, helping someone move, painting, and so on.

While previous chapters focus on celebrating the people who are deeply a part of your life, this chapter pivots to focus on creating community. It is very clear in the Bible that we are not meant to do life alone but in community.

Don't be afraid to invite people you don't know that well—people on your block, folks from church, families from your child's school, whoever. Instead of preparing a whole meal, keep it simple and serve just dessert and coffee. This can help reduce the pressure with people you don't know well. Instead of a long get-together, guests can come and nosh on dessert for just an hour or two.

I am a big fan of the versatility of sheet-pan desserts. If you wind up with more guests than you anticipated, you can cut the pieces smaller or serve generous slices to a more moderate crowd. These sheet-pan desserts are all made in a 13 × 18-inch rimmed sheet pan. If this is too much dessert for your soiree, halve the recipe and make it in a 9 × 13-inch pan.

Eclair

This eclair sheet uses a mixture of "from scratch" elements as well as a few shortcuts to achieve the eclair "essence" without all the fuss of filling and topping individual eclairs. The base is a simple pâte à choux recipe spread thin and baked until crispy. It then gets topped with a rich custard filling that starts with instant vanilla pudding and gets doctored up to take the flavor and richness to the next level. The dessert gets finished with whipped cream and a drizzle of fudge sauce.

ACTIVE TIME: 1 hour | **TOTAL TIME:** 2 hours 15 minutes | **YIELD:** 24 servings (3 × 3-inch squares)

INGREDIENTS

- Pâte à Choux (page 217)
- Fudge Sauce (page 211)

Filling:

- 3 cups whole milk
- ½ cup heavy whipping cream
- 2 (3.4 oz.) pkgs. instant vanilla pudding
- 1 tablespoon vanilla extract
- 1 (8 oz.) pkg. cream cheese, softened

Whipped Cream:

- 3 cups heavy whipping cream
- ¾ cup powdered sugar
- 1 tablespoon vanilla extract

DIRECTIONS

[1] Preheat the oven to 375 degrees.

[2] Prepare the Pâte à Choux according to the recipe directions. Spread the batter using an offset spatula onto an ungreased 13 × 18-inch rimmed baking sheet. Leave a ½-inch gap all the way around the batter so that it has room to expand. Bake for 18 to 22 minutes or until golden. Cool completely.

[3] Prepare the Fudge Sauce according to the recipe directions. Refrigerate until chilled.

[4] Whisk the milk, ½ cup heavy cream, pudding mix, and vanilla for a few minutes until smooth and beginning to thicken. Refrigerate for 30 minutes or until set.

[5] Beat the cream cheese in a stand mixer fitted with the paddle attachment until smooth. Add the vanilla pudding and beat until no streaks remain. Pour the filling over the cooled crust.

[6] Whip the 3 cups heavy cream, powdered sugar, and vanilla in a stand mixer fitted with a whisk attachment until medium peaks form.

[7] Spoon the whipped cream over the pudding and spread it evenly with an offset spatula.

[8] Transfer the fudge sauce to a piping bag. If the sauce is too thick, microwave it for 10 seconds. Snip a small corner of the bag and drizzle it over the whipped cream. Refrigerate until ready to serve. Store leftovers in the fridge.

Sheet Pan Pavlova

Mix up your next gathering with a ginormous fruity pavlova! If you've never had a pavlova, it starts with a meringue that has a crunchy outer layer and is soft in the middle. To balance out the sweetness in the meringue, it's topped with a lightly sweetened whipped cream and loads of fresh fruit. I chose to use blackberries and sliced kiwis, but you can swap them out for whatever fresh fruit you prefer.

ACTIVE TIME: 50 minutes | **TOTAL TIME:** 2 hours 50 minutes | **YIELD:** 24 servings (3 × 3-inch squares)

INGREDIENTS

- 2 batches Sit Back and Relax Meringue (page 217)

Whipped Cream:

- 3 cups heavy whipping cream
- ¾ cup powdered sugar
- 1 tablespoon vanilla extract
- 10 kiwis, peeled and sliced
- 2 (6 oz.) pkgs. fresh blackberries

DIRECTIONS

[1] Preheat the oven to 250 degrees.

[2] Prepare a double batch of Sit Back and Relax Meringue according to the recipe directions.

[3] Dump the meringue onto an ungreased parchment-lined 13 × 18-inch rimmed baking sheet. Use an offset spatula to smooth the meringue into a large rectangle, leaving about a 1-inch gap all the way around the meringue so that it has room to expand. Shape the meringue so that there is a slightly thicker edge to help keep the toppings on. Bake for 1 hour or until the meringue changes from a glossy finish to a matte one. Turn the oven off and crack the door to let the meringue dry out for one more hour. Cool completely.

[4] Beat heavy cream, powdered sugar, and vanilla in a stand mixer fitted with the whisk attachment until soft peaks form.

[5] Scoop whipped cream onto the meringue and spread it into an even layer using an offset spatula. Top with the fruit. Serve immediately. It is best enjoyed the day of. Store leftovers in the refrigerator.

Smoothie Bowl Bars

Sometimes when I write recipes, I picture how you will enjoy them. For this recipe, I picture you and your people sitting on your deck on a hot afternoon, savoring the icy, fruity squares. The kids take a break from the slip-and-slide and have juice running down their chins and arms and big grins on their faces. But even if the picture doesn't look like that—you don't have a deck or a slip-and-slide or kids—these smoothie bowl bars are refreshing and feature all of the best parts of a smoothie bowl in a make-ahead bar form.

ACTIVE TIME: 45 minutes | **TOTAL TIME:** 1 hour 35 minutes | **YIELD:** 24 servings (3 × 3-inch squares)

INGREDIENTS

- 6 cups honey oat granola
- 6 tablespoons salted butter, melted
- ¼ teaspoon salt
- 4 cups frozen dragon fruit
- 4 cups frozen raspberries
- 4 cups frozen strawberries
- 1 (14 oz.) can sweetened condensed milk
- 1 cup pineapple juice

Toppings:

- 3 medium bananas, sliced
- 6 oz. fresh raspberries
- 2 cups sliced fresh strawberries
- ¾ cup honey oat granola
- ½ cup coconut flakes
- ¼ cup roasted and salted pistachios or pepitas
- Honey for drizzling (optional)

DIRECTIONS

[1] Preheat the oven to 350 degrees.

[2] Blitz the 6 cups granola in a food processor until the clusters break down to about oat size. Add the melted butter and salt and stir until combined. Dump the crust onto a 13 × 18-inch rimmed baking sheet. Press the crumbs into a firm layer. Bake for 5 to 7 minutes or until fragrant and browned. Allow it to cool. Freeze until chilled.

[3] Blend the dragon fruit, raspberries, strawberries, sweetened condensed milk, and pineapple juice until smooth. Spread the smoothie over the crust. Freeze for 20 minutes or until the smoothie has firmed up again or until you're ready to serve.

[4] Arrange the toppings over the smoothie and drizzle with honey, if desired. Cut into slices and serve. If the smoothie becomes too soft, pop the pan back in the freezer for 15 to 20 minutes. Store leftovers in the freezer.

TIP: To prevent this from becoming a big soupy mess, you need a high-powered blender (or I use my food processor). Also, most food processors and blenders cannot hold all of the smoothie, so I recommend blending it in 2 to 3 batches and moving each finished batch to the freezer before putting the dessert all together. If at any point it starts melting, pop it in the freezer for 15 to 20 minutes and then continue. You want the crust and the smoothie to be very cold when it all comes together.

Better Than "Better Than ANYTHING Cake"

The "Better Than Anything Cake" has been popular for decades. It's good—really good—but I knew there were several things I could change to level it up, and here's the final result. I scrapped the boxed cake mix and opted for a from-scratch chocolate cake that uses basic pantry ingredients. I also decided to bake the cake in a rimmed sheet pan for a thinner cake and better cake-to-whipped cream ratio. The original recipe calls for both caramel and sweetened condensed milk. It's a total sugar overload. I ditched the sweetened condensed milk, as I felt it added no flavor, just sugar, and opted for my homemade butterscotch sauce instead. I also added ganache to up the flavor game. Instead of whipped topping I whipped up a batch of fresh whipped cream and finished by topping it with the traditional toffee bar chunks.

ACTIVE TIME: 45 minutes | **TOTAL TIME:** 2 hours 55 minutes | **YIELD:** 24 servings (3 × 3-inch squares)

INGREDIENTS

- 2 batches Microwave Butterscotch (page 211)
- 2 batches Chocolate Crazy Cake (page 214)

Ganache:

- 1 cup heavy whipping cream
- 1 cup semisweet chocolate chips

Whipped Cream:

- 3 cups heavy whipping cream
- ¾ cup powdered sugar
- 1 tablespoon vanilla extract
- 4 (1.4 oz.) toffee bars

DIRECTIONS

[1] Prepare the double batch of Microwave Butterscotch according to the recipe directions.

[2] Preheat the oven to 350 degrees.

[3] Prepare a double batch of Chocolate Crazy Cake according to the recipe directions. Pour the batter into a greased 13 × 18-inch rimmed baking sheet. Bake for 15 to 18 minutes or until the cake springs back when gently pressed. Allow it to cool for 10 minutes.

[4] Combine the ganache ingredients in a bowl and microwave for 30 seconds, then stir. Repeat until no lumps remain, about 2 minutes total.

[5] Use the round end of a wooden spoon or spatula to poke holes over the entire surface of the cake. Pour butterscotch over the top of the cake and spread it out using an offset spatula. Pour the ganache on top and spread it evenly. Cover. Refrigerate until chilled, about 2 hours.

[6] Whip the remaining heavy cream with the powdered sugar and vanilla until medium peaks form. Dump whipped cream over the cake and spread in an even layer using an offset spatula.

[7] Chop the toffee bars into small bits. Sprinkle the toffee bits over the cake. Store in the fridge until ready to serve. Store leftovers in the refrigerator.

White Chocolate Blackberry Key Lime Pie

If you're looking for a unique sheet pan dessert to mix up your normal lineup...you found it! I love how the tart blackberry and lime balance with the sweet white chocolate ganache in these super thin flavor-packed squares. If you're in a hurry, forget the white chocolate ganache and blackberries and opt for a simple sheet pan key lime pie. To save time and money I keep a bottle of key lime juice in my fridge ready to make this. I like the Nellie and Joe's brand.

ACTIVE TIME: 35 minutes | **TOTAL TIME:** 3 hours 5 minutes | **YIELD:** 24 servings (3 × 3-inch squares)

INGREDIENTS

Ganache:
- 1 (12 oz.) pkg. white chocolate chips
- 1¾ cups heavy whipping cream, divided

Crust:
- 1 cup salted butter, melted
- 3 cups graham cracker crumbs
- 1 teaspoon salt

Filling:
- 12 large egg yolks
- 1½ cups key lime juice
- 3 (14 oz.) cans sweetened condensed milk

Topping:
- 18 ounces fresh blackberries
- 1 tablespoon lime juice
- 2 tablespoons sugar
- Lime zest for finishing

DIRECTIONS

[1] Heat white chips and ¾ cup of the heavy cream in a microwave-safe dish for 30 seconds. Stir. Heat for another 15 seconds and stir. Repeat if any lumps remain. Refrigerate for about 1 hour, until chilled and thick.

[2] Preheat the oven to 325 degrees.

[3] Toss the butter, graham cracker crumbs, and salt until the crumbs are coated, then press them into the bottom of a 13 × 18-inch rimmed baking sheet. Bake for 8 to 10 minutes or until golden and fragrant.

[4] While the crust is baking, whisk the yolks, 1½ cups lime juice, and sweetened condensed milk until smooth, then pour the mixture over the hot crust. Bake for 18 to 22 minutes or until the filling is set. Allow it to cool and refrigerate until chilled.

[5] Transfer the chilled white chocolate ganache to a stand mixer fitted with the whisk attachment and whip on medium speed until thick and fluffy. Add the remaining 1 cup of heavy cream and whip until thick. Transfer it to a piping bag fitted with a large round tip.

[6] Toss blackberries, 1 tablespoon lime juice, and sugar. Pipe white chocolate dollops in rows, then place a row of blackberries and pipe another row of white chocolate dollops. Leave a gap of about 2 inches and repeat across the top of the pie. Zest a lime over the top. Cut into squares. Serve. Store left-overs in the refrigerator.

Lemon Curd Poke Cake

This can barely be called a cake, as it packs so much lemon curd into this sheet pan. The cake soaks up all the lemony curd, resulting in an extremely moist and flavorful cake. The whipped cream helps balance out the zingy tart flavor. I like to finish the cake with a bit of lemon zest.

ACTIVE TIME: 45 minutes | **TOTAL TIME:** 3 hours | **YIELD:** 24 servings (3 × 3-inch squares)

INGREDIENTS

Cake:

- 1 (13.25 oz) pkg. lemon cake mix
- 1 cup water
- 4 egg whites
- ½ cup canola oil

Lemon Curd:

- 2 batches Lemon Curd (page 212)

Whipped Cream:

- 3 cups heavy whipping cream
- ¾ cup powdered sugar
- 2 teaspoons vanilla extract
- Zest of one lemon

DIRECTIONS

[1] Preheat the oven to 325 degrees.

[2] Whisk the cake mix, water, egg whites, and oil in a medium-size bowl until smooth.

[3] Pour the batter into a greased 13 × 18-inch rimmed baking sheet. Bake for 12 to 15 minutes or until the cake springs back when gently pressed.

[4] While the cake is baking, prepare the double batch of Lemon Curd according to the recipe directions.

[5] When the cake is removed from the oven, allow it to cool for 5 minutes. Use the end of a wooden spoon or your gloved hand to poke holes over the entire surface of the cake. Pour the still warm lemon curd over the top of the cake and use an offset spatula to spread it out. Cover. Refrigerate until chilled, about 2 hours.

[6] Whip the heavy cream, powdered sugar, and vanilla until medium peaks form. Dump the cream over the curd and spread evenly using an offset spatula. Zest a lemon over the top. Cut into squares. Serve. Store leftovers in the fridge.

Roasted Strawberry Rhubarb Cheesecake

What would happen if a no-bake cheesecake and a strawberry rhubarb crumble had a baby? You would get this strawberry rhubarb no-bake cheesecake! Here's the process: bake a giant oatmeal cookie, break it up, toss the crumbs with melted butter, press into a sheet pan, top with no-bake cheesecake, roast and cool a juicy strawberry rhubarb topping, and spread it over the top. The result is a lovely symphony of salty and oaty flavors with sour fruit and creamy, rich filling.

ACTIVE TIME: 50 minutes | **TOTAL TIME:** 2 hours 15 minutes | **YIELD:** 24 servings (3 × 3-inches)

INGREDIENTS

Topping:

- 2 lbs. fresh strawberries
- 3 cups chopped rhubarb (½ to 1-inch pieces)
- ⅔ cup powdered sugar

Crust:

- ¾ cup salted butter, softened
- ⅔ cup dark brown sugar
- ¼ cup sugar
- 2 large eggs
- 1¾ cups old-fashioned oats
- 1 cup all-purpose flour
- ½ teaspoon salt
- ¼ teaspoon baking powder
- ¼ teaspoon baking soda
- 1 cup salted butter, melted

Filling:

- 3 (8 oz.) pkgs. cream cheese, softened
- 3 cups powdered sugar
- 3 cups heavy whipping cream
- 1 tablespoon vanilla extract

DIRECTIONS

[1] Preheat the oven to 400 degrees.

[2] *Prepare the topping.* Hull and halve the strawberries (chop larger ones into quarters). Toss strawberries, rhubarb, and powdered sugar on a parchment-lined baking sheet. Bake for 15 to 20 minutes or until the rhubarb is tender but not broken down. Transfer to a storage container and refrigerate until chilled.

[3] *Prepare the oat cookie crust.* While the fruit is roasting, cream softened butter, brown sugar, and sugar in a stand mixer fitted with a paddle attachment until fluffy. Add eggs and mix until combined. Add oats, flour, salt, baking powder, and baking soda until combined. Dump the dough onto a greased and parchment-lined 13 × 18-inch rimmed baking sheet and spread it until it is about ¼ inch thick. Once the fruit is out of the oven, reduce the temperature to 350 degrees. Bake the crust for 12 to 14 minutes or until golden. Cool completely.

[4] Break the giant oat cookie into chunks and blitz it in the food processor until it is broken into crumbs. Toss the crumbs with the cup of melted butter and press into a 13 × 18-inch rimmed baking sheet. Pop the crust in the freezer until you are ready to fill it.

[5] *Make the filling and assemble your cheesecake.* Cream the cream cheese and powdered sugar in a stand mixer fitted with a paddle attachment until smooth. Add the heavy cream and vanilla and beat until combined. Swap the paddle attachment for the whisk attachment and whip until thick. Dump the filling on the crust and spread it into an even layer using an offset spatula. Spoon the roasted compote over the top and gently spread the fruit using the back of a spoon. For clean-cut squares, refrigerate for 1 hour to allow the cream to set. Cut into squares and serve. Store leftovers in the refrigerator.

Hula Pie

My sister Ann flew to Hawaii on a work assignment (obviously Ann is not a teacher), and my sister Susan and I tagged along and enjoyed all the perks of a free and fancy hotel—emphasis on the free. We visited Duke's, a famous Hawaiian restaurant serving up monstrous slices of this incredible Hula Pie. Needless to say, in the short week we were there, we became regulars. There's a reason this pie is so famous. The crunchy Oreo crust and salty macadamia nuts contrast with the rich fudge and fluffy whipped cream. I converted all the flavors of the pie into a sheet pan, and man, this tastes just like the real thing.

ACTIVE TIME: 50 minutes | **TOTAL TIME:** 2 hours 5 minutes | **YIELD:** 24 servings (3 × 3-inch squares)

INGREDIENTS

- 3 batches Fudge Sauce (page 211)
- 12 oz. salted and roasted macadamia nuts, divided
- 1 (18.12 oz.) pkg. Oreos (family size)
- ½ cup salted butter, melted
- 1 gallon vanilla ice cream, softened

Whipped Cream:

- 2 cups heavy whipping cream
- ½ cup powdered sugar
- 2 teaspoons vanilla extract

DIRECTIONS

[1] Preheat the oven to 350 degrees.

[2] Prepare the triple batch of Fudge Sauce. Refrigerate until chilled.

[3] Chop the macadamia nuts. Divide in half.

[4] Blitz the Oreos in a food processor or throw them in a gallon bag and use a rolling pin to crush them until they are fine crumbs. Add melted butter and stir until combined. Dump the crumbs onto a 13 × 18-inch rimmed baking sheet. Press the crumbs into a firm layer. Bake for 10 minutes. Cool completely.

[5] Mix ice cream and half of the nuts in a large bowl until combined. Dump the ice cream over the crust and spread it into an even layer. If you're struggling to get the ice cream to spread, put a piece of plastic wrap over the top and use your hands to press over the plastic into an even layer. Freeze for 15 minutes. Pour the fudge over the top and spread it in an even layer. Work quickly, as the fudge will start to set up. Sprinkle the remaining macadamia nuts on top. Freeze for at least another 10 minutes.

[6] When you're ready to serve, whip the heavy cream, powdered sugar, and vanilla in a stand mixer fitted with a whisk attachment until stiff peaks form. Transfer to a piping bag fitted with a star tip.

[7] Pipe squiggles of whipped cream across the fudge and cut into squares. Serve. Store leftovers in an airtight container.

Banoffee Pie

Banoffee Pie is a no-bake dessert named for combining bananas and "toffee." The dessert originates from Britain and features a salty graham cracker crust, dulce de leche, banana slices, whipped cream, and grated bittersweet chocolate. The dulce de leche on its own is too sweet, but the crust, bananas, and dark chocolate work together to balance out the flavors. Because it is a rich dessert, I like to serve small pieces, which means this sheet pan will serve a serious crowd! The metal offset spatula is a key piece of equipment in this recipe. If you try to use a rubber spatula, the banana slices and dulce de leche will drift all over the place and turn into a hot mess.

ACTIVE TIME: 30 minutes | **TOTAL TIME:** 40 minutes | **YIELD:** 36 servings (2 × 3-inch rectangles)

INGREDIENTS

Crust:

- 3 cups graham cracker crumbs
- 1 cup salted butter, melted
- ½ cup sugar
- 1 teaspoon salt

Filling:

- 7 to 8 ripe but firm bananas
- 4 (13.4 oz.) cans dulce de leche

Whipped Cream:

- 3 cups heavy whipping cream
- 1 cup powdered sugar
- 1 tablespoon vanilla extract
- 1 oz. bittersweet chocolate

DIRECTIONS

[1] Toss the graham cracker crumbs, butter, sugar, and salt. Press into the bottom of a 13 × 18-inch rimmed baking sheet. Refrigerate for 10 minutes.

[2] While the crust is chilling, peel and slice the bananas about ¼ inch thick and open the cans of dulce de leche.

[3] Spoon 2 cans of dulce de leche over the crust. Use an offset spatula to spread it in a very thin layer. Place slices of bananas over the dulce de leche about one-fourth to one-half inch apart. Use your hands to press the banana slices down.

[4] Spoon the remaining 2 cans of dulce de leche over the top and spread in an even layer using an offset spatula.

[5] Whip the heavy cream, powdered sugar, and vanilla until medium peaks form. Dump the whipped cream on top and spread evenly. Grate the chocolate over the top using the smaller holes on your cheese grater. Serve. Store leftovers in the fridge.

Vanilla Raspberry Poke Cake

One June, I asked my five-year-old brother Seth what kind of cake he wanted for his birthday. I was expecting an answer like "Thomas the Train" or "Cars" or something along those lines, but instead he said, "Vanilla Raspberry Cake!" Best answer ever. This cake is inspired by the vanilla raspberry cupcakes that I used to make for weddings, which were by far my most popular flavor. I've made thousands of this cupcake flavor alone—seriously, it's popular! I now prefer the sheet cake because it's easier and faster. And not to be nerdy about this, but because it's a sheet, every single bite has the perfect ratio of cake, filling, and frosting. You don't have to get to the middle of the cupcake to hit the filling or get more frosting in certain bites. Like I said, nerdy but real.

ACTIVE TIME: 45 minutes | **TOTAL TIME:** 3 hours | **YIELD:** 24 servings (3 × 3-inch squares)

INGREDIENTS

- Vanilla Doctored Cake Mix (page 214)
- Two-Ingredient Raspberry Filling (page 213)
- Vanilla Whipped Frosting (page 215)
- 12 oz. fresh raspberries

DIRECTIONS

[1] Preheat the oven to 325 degrees.

[2] Prepare Vanilla Doctored Cake Mix according to the recipe directions. Pour the batter into a greased 13 × 18-inch rimmed baking sheet. Bake for 13 to 16 minutes or until the cake springs back when gently pressed. Allow the cake to cool for 10 minutes.

[3] While the cake is baking, prepare the Two-Ingredient Raspberry Filling according to the recipe directions.

[4] Use the round end of a wooden spoon or a spatula to poke holes over the entire surface of the cake. Pour raspberry filling over the top of the cake and use an offset spatula to spread it out. Cover. Refrigerate until chilled, about 2 hours.

[5] Prepare the Vanilla Whipped Frosting according to the recipe directions. Spoon frosting over the filling and spread evenly using an offset spatula. Place the raspberries on top. Serve. Store leftovers in the fridge.

The Only Party Game You Will Ever Need!

Like I said earlier, my family are all big "visit-ers." We love to gab, but even so there is a noticeable difference when you get a group of people playing this game. They start loosening up, laughing, and when the game is finished there's a noticeable camaraderie and comfortability among the group. This will forever be my family's go-to party game for any occasion. Some people call this game fishbowl or salad bowl.

Materials

All you need are lots of small slips of paper (about 3 to 4 per person), writing utensils, and a big bowl (plastic is probably the safest).

Getting Going

Pick a theme—it can be anything. We often pick a theme based on the time of year like Christmas, "back to school," summertime, and so on. Each person gets a few slips and writes three things that have to do with the theme. It's easiest if everyone does nouns so, "person, place, or thing." After people finish writing their words they can fold their slips in half and throw them in the bowl without anyone seeing what they wrote. Split your guests into two teams. It's easiest if people move to be near their group. You need someone to be the timer. We usually just use our phones and set a timer for 30 seconds. You also need a scorekeeper. Each slip is worth a point.

Round 1: Describe the word(s) on the slip with any words except the ones on the slip.

Round 2: Charades, which is pretty self-explanatory, is just getting people to guess by acting out (not using any words) what is written on the slip.

Round 3: You can say only one word to get them to guess the secret word. It sounds like it would be impossible to get people to guess with only one word, but everyone has heard all of the words in the bowl twice by the time you get to the third round.

Alternate 30-second turns between each team until the bowl is empty. Each person is trying to get through as many slips as possible in 30 seconds. They may not get any, or they may get five guessed. As the words are guessed, remove them from the bowl. When the bowl is empty, the round is over. Put all the slips back in the bowl and move on to the next round.

Whichever team has the most points (words guessed) at the end of three rounds wins!

CHAPTER 10

Not So Basic "Basics"

The buzz term "capsule wardrobe" has been a topic in the fashion space for quite some time—mostly because it only makes sense to mix and match favorite pieces to create different outfits. It's not really born from a trend but from common sense. I love to apply this concept to baking and desserts too. Basic cake, pastry, filling, and frosting recipes can be mixed and matched into many combinations.

The recipes in this chapter have been referenced throughout the book to be combined into various treats. Feel free to take these recipes and run with them as foundational "pieces" to mix and match into new creations. The more you make these recipes, the faster you will get, and the easier it will be to make them repeatedly in different ways.

Fudge Sauce

This fudge sauce takes the basic chocolate ganache to the next level by adding butter and corn syrup for a glossy finish and extra-rich flavor. Swap in milk chocolate chips instead of semisweet if you prefer a sweeter sauce.

ACTIVE TIME: 5 minutes | **TOTAL TIME:** 5 minutes | **YIELD:** ⅔ cup

INGREDIENTS

- ½ cup semisweet chocolate chips
- ¼ cup heavy whipping cream
- 1 tablespoon salted butter
- 1 tablespoon corn syrup

DIRECTIONS

[1] Heat the fudge ingredients in a microwave-safe dish for 30 seconds and stir. If any lumps remain, heat for another 30 seconds and stir until smooth. Store leftovers in the fridge.

Microwave Butterscotch

Caramel can be finicky to make, as it crystalizes easily and must be cooked to a precise temperature—not too hot, not too cold. Enter the butterscotch syrup. It's very forgiving and painless to whip together. Not to mention that the molasses flavor from the brown sugar and the addition of the butter add a depth of flavor you just won't find in caramel sauce.

ACTIVE TIME: 10 minutes | **TOTAL TIME:** 10 minutes | **YIELD:** 1½ cups

INGREDIENTS

- ½ cup salted butter, melted
- 1 cup dark brown sugar
- ¼ cup water
- 2 tablespoons corn syrup
- ¼ cup heavy whipping cream
- 1 teaspoon vanilla extract
- ½ teaspoon salt

DIRECTIONS

[1] Whisk butter, brown sugar, water, and corn syrup for 1 minute. Microwave for 1 minute. Stir and repeat. Continue cooking for 1-minute intervals until the mixture comes to a boil.

[2] Add the heavy cream, vanilla, and salt and stir until smooth. Store in the refrigerator.

NOTE: If your butterscotch syrup separates while in the refrigerator, simply heat it in the microwave for 20 seconds and give it a whisk until it comes back together in a homogenous mixture.

Lemon Curd

This curd is tangy yet rich and thick. It can be served over cake, inside crepes, or eaten off a spoon. It seems fancy but couldn't be easier to make.

ACTIVE TIME: 10 minutes | **TOTAL TIME:** 2 hours 10 minutes | **YIELD:** 2 cups

INGREDIENTS

- ½ cup salted butter
- 1 cup sugar
- ⅔ cup lemon juice
- 5 egg yolks

DIRECTIONS

[1] Heat butter for 30 to 40 seconds or until melted in a large microwave-safe bowl.

[2] Add the sugar and whisk until combined. Add the lemon juice and egg yolks and whisk until smooth. Microwave for 1 minute. Stir. Repeat. Microwave for a total of 4 minutes or until slightly thickened and foamy on top. It should be the consistency of gravy. Check the consistency by dipping a spoon in the curd. Draw a line through the curd on the back of the spoon. If the spoon remains visible, it is thick enough. If the curd runs back together, continue to microwave it at 1-minute intervals until it reaches this stage. It will continue to thicken as it chills.

[3] Strain with a mesh sieve. Pour into a storage container and press plastic wrap to the surface to prevent it from forming a skin. Chill for 2 to 3 hours or until thick. Store in the refrigerator.

Two-Ingredient Raspberry Filling

Most fruit compotes are cooked and thickened with cornstarch. Cooking the succulent fruit can result in losing a lot of the fresh, zingy flavor. So, in this recipe, I only cook half of the fruit and use a bit of Jell-O to thicken the mixture and brighten back up any lost raspberry flavor.

ACTIVE TIME: 10 minutes | **TOTAL TIME:** 1 hour 10 minutes | **YIELD:** 3 cups

INGREDIENTS

- 24 oz. frozen raspberries
- 1 (3 oz.) pkg. raspberry Jell-O

DIRECTIONS

[1] Dump about half of the frozen raspberries into a microwave-safe dish, defrost the raspberries until thawed (about 2 minutes on defrost, depending on your microwave), then heat the raspberries until hot and bubbly (about 2 minutes, depending on your microwave).

[2] Add the Jell-O and stir until dissolved.

[3] Dump in the remaining frozen raspberries and stir. Blend using an immersion blender until smooth.

[4] Cover and refrigerate the filling for 1 to 2 hours or until thick. Store in the refrigerator.

NOTE: If you pull the filling out of the fridge and it has turned into one big gelatinous blob, don't panic! Add a tablespoon or two of hot water and stir until smooth.

Coconut Cream

This not-too-sweet coconut cream is thick and ultra versatile. It can be thrown in a pie (page 93), piped into donuts (page 179), or layered between crepes (page 38). This custard is naturally gluten-free, so if you have family members or guests who need this option, coconut cream can be layered in a parfait glass or served over a gluten-free pie crust and topped with whipped cream.

ACTIVE TIME: 20 minutes | **TOTAL TIME:** 1 hour 20 minutes | **YIELD:** About 4 cups

INGREDIENTS

- 1 (14 oz.) can full-fat coconut milk
- 1 cup whole milk
- ⅔ cup sugar, divided
- ½ cup unsweetened coconut flakes
- Pinch of salt
- 6 egg yolks
- ¼ cup cornstarch
- 2 tablespoons butter
- 1 teaspoon vanilla extract
- 1 teaspoon coconut extract

DIRECTIONS

[1] Heat the coconut milk, milk, ⅓ cup sugar, coconut, and salt in a medium-size bowl in the microwave until steamy, but DO NOT boil, about 2 minutes.

[2] While that is heating, whisk the remaining sugar, egg yolks, and cornstarch in a small bowl until smooth.

[3] Slowly stream about ½ cup of the hot milk mixture into the eggs, whisking constantly until smooth. This will slowly bring the eggs up to temperature (this process is called tempering). Pour the now-tempered eggs into the rest of the hot milk stirring all the while.

[4] Heat in the microwave for 2 minutes, stirring in between, about 4 to 6 minutes. Look for it to be the consistency of pudding or yogurt. Once thick, add the butter, vanilla, and coconut extract. Stir until the butter has melted. Allow to cool slightly. Cover with plastic wrap, pressing it to the surface to prevent a skin from forming. Refrigerate for 1 to 2 hours until chilled. Store leftovers in the fridge.

Vanilla Doctored Cake Mix

Sometimes you just need an easy win, and this doctored cake mix is just that. It takes the basic cake mix and ups the moisture with the addition of sour cream and swaps whole eggs for egg whites, creating a tender, light, and moist cake that can be eaten on its own, layered in a cake, or used as the foundation for a poke cake.

ACTIVE TIME: 5 minutes | **TOTAL TIME:** 25 minutes | **YIELD:** 2 (8 inch) round cakes or 1 (13 x 18 inch) sheet cake

INGREDIENTS

- 1 cup water
- ½ cup sour cream
- ½ cup canola oil
- 4 egg whites
- 1 tablespoon vanilla extract
- 1 (13.25 oz.) pkg. French vanilla cake mix

DIRECTIONS

[1] Preheat the oven to 325 degrees.

[2] Whisk the water, sour cream, oil, egg whites, and vanilla in a medium-size mixing bowl until smooth.

[3] Add the cake mix and whisk until smooth and thick.

[4] Pour into your desired pan and bake as follows until the cake springs back when gently pressed: bake two 8-inch round pans for 18 to 20 minutes, or one 13 × 18-inch pan for 15 to 18 minutes.

[5] Cool completely. Store leftovers in an airtight container.

Chocolate Crazy Cake

This depression-era cake uses pantry ingredients to yield a sturdy chocolate cake that can be used in many applications. This cake recipe gets bonus points for being egg free and dairy free.

ACTIVE TIME: 5 minutes | **TOTAL TIME:** 35 minutes | **YIELD:** 1 (8 inch) round cake or 1 thin (9 × 13 inch) cake

INGREDIENTS

- 1½ cups all-purpose flour
- 1 cup sugar
- ½ cup cocoa powder
- 1 teaspoon baking soda
- ½ teaspoon salt
- 1 cup cold water
- ⅓ cup canola oil
- 1 teaspoon distilled white vinegar
- 1 teaspoon vanilla extract

DIRECTIONS

[1] Preheat the oven to 350 degrees.

[2] Whisk flour, sugar, cocoa powder, baking soda, and salt in a medium-size mixing bowl.

[3] Add water, oil, vinegar, and vanilla and whisk until combined. You might see a few lumps, and that's okay. Pour the batter into a greased and parchment-lined baking pan of your choice. Bake as follows until the cake springs back when gently pressed: bake one 8-inch round pan for 25 to 30 minutes, or one 9 × 13-inch rectangle pan for 15 to 18 minutes.

[4] Cool completely. Store leftovers in an airtight container.

Chocolate Whipped Cream

This chocolate whipped cream uses pantry staples like powdered sugar, cocoa powder, and vanilla to amp up heavy whipping cream into a smooth and chocolatey cream that can be used to finish a dessert, frost a cake, or serve it with a spoon and call it chocolate mousse!

ACTIVE TIME: 10 minutes | **TOTAL TIME:** 10 minutes | **YIELD:** About 4 cups

INGREDIENTS

- 2 cups heavy whipping cream
- 1½ cups powdered sugar
- ½ cup cocoa powder
- 1 teaspoon vanilla extract

DIRECTIONS

[1] Whip the heavy cream, powdered sugar, cocoa, and vanilla in a stand mixer fitted with a whisk attachment until medium peaks form. Use immediately. Store leftovers in the fridge.

Vanilla Whipped Frosting

My aunt has made numerous wedding cakes and got tired of using a sickly sweet buttercream and instead started to use a whipped cream product from a restaurant supply store. It wasn't really whipped cream, but it was slightly sweet, light, and very sturdy. She would often give me a quart or two when she had an order, and it was fantastic, but eventually, we were not able to get it, and at the end of the day, it wasn't really whipped cream; it was corn syrup, oil, and gums. I developed this recipe to produce a similar result: thick, fluffy, and sturdy. One of my favorite things about this recipe is that you can adjust the sugar without losing the texture. If you reduce the sugar in buttercream, it will not be thick enough, but in this recipe, you have free rein to increase or decrease the powdered sugar.

ACTIVE TIME: 15 minutes | **TOTAL TIME:** 15 minutes | **YIELD:** About 4 cups

INGREDIENTS

- 1 (8 oz.) pkg. cream cheese, softened
- 1 cup powdered sugar
- 2 teaspoons vanilla extract
- 2 cups heavy whipping cream, chilled

DIRECTIONS

[1] Beat the cream cheese in a stand mixer fitted with a paddle attachment on low speed until smooth.

[2] Add the powdered sugar and vanilla. Beat until smooth and there are no remaining lumps. Scrape the bowl to ensure no bits of cream cheese are stuck on the bottom or sides.

[3] Add the heavy cream and beat until smooth. Remove the paddle attachment and swap in the whisk attachment and whip until thick. If you pull the bowl off the mixer and tilt the bowl on its side, the frosting should stay put. If it's still loose enough to move around, keep whipping. Use the frosting immediately! Store leftovers in the refrigerator.

Sit Back and Relax Meringue

Many meringue recipes require babysitting the meringue and slowly adding the sugar as it mixes—not this one. Adding all of the sugar at the beginning, starting on a slow speed, and gradually increasing it gives the sugar time to dissolve without having to stand over the mixer the whole time. But if you have a hand mixer, you can retitle this recipe "Stand Up and Hold Meringue." One crucial step is to allow your egg whites to come to room temperature. For best results, separate your eggs while they're cold and allow the egg whites to sit at room temperature for 30 to 40 minutes or longer if your kitchen is particularly chilly.

ACTIVE TIME: 5 minutes | **TOTAL TIME:** 35 minutes | **YIELD:** About 4 cups

INGREDIENTS

- 4 large egg whites at room temperature
- 1 cup sugar
- ½ teaspoon cream of tartar
- ½ teaspoon vanilla extract
- Pinch of salt

DIRECTIONS

[1] Add all the meringue ingredients to a stand mixer fitted with a whisk attachment. Start the mixer on the lowest speed, gradually increasing the speed about every 5 minutes. Stop and scrape the bowl occasionally.

[2] It will take 20 to 30 minutes to get to the proper stage. A few key things to look for are, first, a thick, glossy meringue; second, if you take a bit of the meringue between your fingers, it should be smooth without any grittiness. Use immediately with any recipe that calls for meringue.

Pâte à Choux

This simple pastry can be used to create a variety of impressive desserts like the Paris-Brest (page 109) or the sheet pan Eclair (page 193). The eggs in this batter cause this pastry to puff up and create a crunchy exterior and custardy interior.

ACTIVE TIME: 20 minutes | **TOTAL TIME:** 25 minutes | **YIELD:** 1 batch

INGREDIENTS

- 1 cup water
- ½ cup salted butter
- 1 cup all-purpose flour
- 2 teaspoons sugar
- 4 large eggs

DIRECTIONS

[1] Heat the water and butter in a small saucepan over medium-low heat until the butter is melted and the mixture starts to boil.

[2] Add the flour and the sugar. Stir vigorously with a spatula until the batter comes off the sides of the pan and forms a ball. This will take about a minute.

[3] Transfer the batter to a medium-size mixing bowl or stand mixer bowl and cool for 5 minutes.

[4] Add the eggs one at a time and whisk until completely smooth and no lumps remain. At first, it will seem like the mixture won't come together, but keep whisking until the batter is very sticky and when you pull the whisk out of the bowl the batter stretches and doesn't immediately break. Use immediately with any recipe that calls for choux pastry.

Crepes

The first recipe I ever wrote was for crepes, in the second grade. My country school classroom was making a classroom cookbook. Our teacher, Mrs. Lyon, asked each student to write a recipe...on their own. We didn't run home and ask our moms for a recipe. Instead, we just made them up, so you can imagine that the recipes in this cookbook didn't get used much. I had just seen crepes for the first time on the cover of a Taste of Home *cooking magazine, and they looked so yummy, filled with whipped cream and fruit. So I attempted to write a crepe recipe. I don't remember much about it other than I directed people to roll the dough out using a rolling pin! Needless to say, the recipe was never going to produce crepes. Since then I have definitely mastered the crepe. If you use a nonstick pan to cook your crepes, you won't need to grease your pan between each crepe. Typically, I spray a bit of nonstick cooking spray before the first crepe, and after that, I don't use any more cooking spray. If you aren't using a nonstick pan, lightly grease the pan with nonstick cooking spray or butter between each crepe.*

ACTIVE TIME: 35 minutes | **TOTAL TIME:** 55 minutes | **YIELD:** About 20 crepes

INGREDIENTS

- 1½ cups whole milk
- 4 tablespoons salted butter, melted
- 4 large eggs
- 1 cup all-purpose flour
- 2 tablespoons sugar

DIRECTIONS

[1] Add the milk, melted butter, eggs, flour, and sugar to a medium-size bowl. Blend using an immersion blender until smooth. Cover and refrigerate for 20 minutes.

[2] Heat an 8-inch nonstick skillet over medium-high heat.

[3] Remove the batter from the fridge and whisk it to make sure that no flour settled.

[4] Pour about 3 tablespoons of batter into the center of the pan. Swirl the batter quickly, allowing it to coat the bottom of the pan. Cook for about 45 seconds or until the edges start to brown and get crispy.

[5] Loosen the edges of the crepe using a rubber spatula and flip. Allow to cook for 15 to 20 seconds more. Remove using a spatula.

[6] Cook the rest of the crepes. As you remove each crepe from the pan, stack them on a dinner plate, layering a small piece of parchment paper between each of them so that they do not get stuck together. Allow to cool completely. Serve immediately or store covered in the fridge until ready to use.

NOTE: Crepes can take a little trial and error as you start. Just like pancakes, the first is usually not that great. The crepes should be light in color with light brown edges and a few brown spots on the crepe. If they are set before you can swirl the batter to the edges of the pan, reduce the heat.

[ACKNOWLEDGMENTS]

To my internet friends, this would never have been possible without you! When I was a young girl, I dreamed of writing a cookbook, but I didn't think I would ever be able to do that. When I started sharing content in 2020 in hopes of someday writing a cookbook, it still seemed so far beyond reach. But over time, one by one, you showed up and showered me with kindness, encouragement, and support. Each time you shared how you made one of my recipes, it blew me away. I would think, "People are actually making these recipes!" It's still my favorite part of sharing recipes!

To my recipe testers: When I put a call out for recipe testers, I got an email that said, "You're telling me I have to buy the ingredients with my own money, follow the recipe exactly, write out detailed feedback…and there's no pay?" And they were right. It wasn't a very lucrative deal, but despite that, so many of you came through for me, and you are the real MVPs of this cookbook. You helped me clarify the wording and let me know when things were not working. I couldn't have written this cookbook without my testers. Thank you! And to my sister Ann for heading up the whole testing crew: It was no small feat to manage.

To my agent Joy, none of this would have been possible without you! Thank you for being willing to represent me and this idea. You know how to make things happen, and I appreciate your encouragement and support throughout the process.

To Ruth, Heather, and the Harvest House team. Thank you for catching the vision and allowing me to write this book with you.

To my students, past, present, and future, it is a joy to be your teacher! You have made my life so much better and brought laughter to the mundane. Don't forget—you are a difference-maker!

To my village people: Monica Coyle, Vicki Hahn, Iris Day, Mrs. Lyon, Miss Hettich, Coach VanZee, Mrs. Hewitt, Dr. Lundgren, Michelle Stockert, and Becca Ford. Thank you for teaching, mentoring, and encouraging me.

To my family: Grandad, Grandma, Papa, Grandma, Linda, Erling, Lisa, and Unc. Thank you for showing up and loving me every step along the way. You are dear to me.

To my siblings: Ann, Tricia, Susan, Lindsey, Josh, and Seth. You bring joy and purpose to my life. There's no one else I would rather walk through life with.

To Mom and Dad, thank you for everything. I love you.

Jesus, none of this is my doing. This is You. Thank You for this great gift! I know that everything good is from You, and writing this cookbook has been such a sweet gift. Most of all, thank You for the gift of salvation, which allows me to walk through each day, no matter how difficult, filled with peace and joy. You are a good God, and I love You.

[INDEX]

Almond Croissant Blondies 157
Almond Wedding Cake 67
Apple Galette 64
Apple Strudel 171
Banoffee Pie 205
Berry Roll Cake 110
Better Than "Better Than ANYTHING Cake" 197
Biscoff Coffee Banana Pudding 161
Black Forest Meringue Cake 31
Blender Chocolate Mousse 72
Blueberry Crumble Coffee Cake 178
Blueberry Swirl Cheesecake 94
Browned Butter Malted Chunk Cookies 162
Cake Batter Ice Cream Cake 49
Cardamom Fig Bar 152
Chantilly Vanilla Cream Puff 59
Cherry Almond Crumble 57
Chocolate Crazy Cake 214
Chocolate Crazy Cake with Penuche Frosting 85
Chocolate Orange Bostock 175
Chocolate Raspberry Waffle Cake 42
Chocolate Revel Bars 86
Chocolate Shell Crème 71
Chocolate Whipped Cream 215
Cinnamon Dulce Ice Cream Pint 60
Cinnamon Oatmeal Cream Pies 165
Coconut Almond Crepe Cake 38
Coconut Cream 213
Coconut Cream Cake 32
Coconut Cream Pie 93
Coconut Croissant 188
Crepes 218
Daddy's Favorite Gingersnaps 80
Decadent Chocolate Cake 68
Double Dutch Baby 182
Eclair 193
Elevated Dump Bars 90
Fancy Cake 106
Fudge Sauce 211
Funeral Bars 87
Grand Chocolate Towers 114
Granola Blondies 158
Hula Pie 204
Lemon Blueberry Cornbread Loaf 151
Lemon Curd 212
Lemon Curd Poke Cake 201
Lemony Fruit Pizzas 131
Macerated Blackberries with Caramelized Pound Cake 136
Mango Fool 143
Maple Brown Butter Cinnamon Rolls 186
Maple Brown Sugar Whipped Coffee Float 133
Microwave Butterscotch 211
Mocha Silk Pie Cake 46
Molasses Bananas Foster 142
Nanaimo Bars 140
Not So Extreme Oreo Cheesecake 104
Parent Trap Ice Cream Cake 45
Paris-Brest 109
Pâte à Choux 217

Peaches and Cream Angel Food "Torn"ado 135
Peanut Butter Bars 91
Peanut Butter Chocolate Chip Snacking Cake 166
Peanut Butter S'mores Baked Alaska 113
Pineapple Puff Pastry Tart 119
Pistachio Crunch Cake 37
Pistachio Faux Fried Ice Cream 139
Pumpkin Crumble Coffee Cake 185
Pumpkin Roll 89
Raspberry Almond Cupcakes 123
Raspberry Crusted Pound Cake 120
Rhubarb Custard Crumb Cake 97
Ritz Crispy S'mores Bars 159
Roasted Strawberry Rhubarb Cheesecake 202
Salty Cracker Peanut Butter Pie 129
Scotcheroo Bundt 121
Sheet Pan Pavlova 194
Shortcut Chocolate Whoopie Pies 155
Shortcut Coconut Malasadas 179
Shortcut Raspberry Kuchen 79
Sit Back and Relax Meringue 217
Smoothie Bowl Bars 195
Smothered Blueberry Lemon Scones 176
Speedy Chocolate Cake 132
Strawberry Cheesecake Napoleon 63
Strawberry Coconut Cake 41
Strawberry Fondue Bowls 128
Strawberry Shortcake 82
Summery Panna Cotta 61
Take 5 Ice Cream Sundae Cones 145
Tiramisu Icebox Cake 33
Triple Layer Carrot Cake 34
Two-Ingredient Raspberry Filling 213
Ultimate Almond Poppy Seed Muffins 172
Vanilla Doctored Cake Mix 214
Vanilla Raspberry Poke Cake 206
Vanilla Whipped Frosting 215
White Chocolate Blackberry Key Lime Pie 198
White Chocolate Mocha Toffee Trifle 117
White Chocolate Raspberry Crepe Platter 181

ABOUT THE AUTHOR

Katie Lee Wilken is a high school math teacher, a summer ranch hand on her family's property, and a year-round dessert content creator. She's been passionate about baking since childhood, when she started learning in the kitchen with her grandma, and she's always loved diving into cookbooks for inspiration. Beyond sharing delicious recipes, Katie's mission is rooted in her Christian faith—she believes every person is valuable, created by God, and deserving of celebration. Through her sweet creations, she encourages others to bless those around them and make them feel special.